THE CIRCLE (

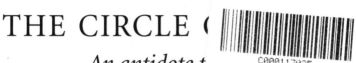

An antidote t

Ken Lewis
and
Trevor Dennis

First published in Great Britain in 2015

Society for Promoting Christian Knowledge
36 Causton Street
London SW1P 4ST
www.spck.org.uk

British Library Cataloguing-in-Publication Data
A catalogue record for this book is available from the British Library

ISBN 978–0–281–07211–8
eBook ISBN 978–0–281–07212–5

Typeset by Graphicraft Limited, Hong Kong
First printed in Great Britain by Ashford Colour Press
Subsequently digitally printed in Great Britain

eBook by Graphicraft Limited, Hong Kong

Produced on paper from sustainable forests

For Janis and Caroline

Second Commandment

Love your neighbour as yourself.
The trouble is, we do.
And since we do not always love ourselves,
Our neighbour suffers from our handicap.
Strange feelings come from depths we don't
Control, causing us to react, and not respond.
How can we learn to love our dark unknown,
Embrace, accept, forgive what lies within?
Can we believe it is already done?
We are profoundly loved, both in our depths
And to the limit of his love, which has no end.
A starting place, with time and then eternity
To learn its truth. And, in the meantime,
What a blessing for our neighbour, to be
Loved as we (are learning to) love ourselves.

Ann Lewin

Contents

About the authors

Ken Lewis is a chartered psychologist with the British Psychological Society. Until his retirement, he held a practitioner certificate in counselling and occupational psychology. He was the first person in the UK to be accredited as a cognitive behavioural therapy (CBT) practitioner, and practised as a therapist for over thirty years. For ten years, he led the postgraduate diploma and MSc courses in CBT at Chester University. Currently, he is an accreditor for the British Association for Behavioural and Cognitive Psychotherapies. Ken is a member of St Michael's Church, Plas Newton in Chester and of the Chester Diocese Mental Health Forum. In equal measure, he is enthusiastic about riding his motorcycle, sailing and jazz. He is married to Janis and they have two grown-up sons.

Trevor Dennis taught Old Testament Studies at Salisbury and Wells (now Sarum) Theological College for twelve years, before taking up the post of Canon Chancellor at Chester Cathedral, where he later became Vice Dean. Over the years, he has published 12 books for SPCK, as well as a children's Bible, *The Book of Books*, for Lion Hudson. He retired in 2010 but continues to be in demand all over the country as a speaker to Christian groups from many denominations. He is married to Caroline and they have four children and six grandchildren.

Acknowledgements

We are very grateful to Ann Lewin for giving us permission to use her wonderful poem 'Second Commandment' as a preface to this book, and for doing so in such a gracious and generous manner.

Dr Lynn Mackie, who is both a theologian and a therapist (she is Programme Leader for the Postgraduate Diploma and MSc in Cognitive Behavioural Psychotherapies at Bolton University), read and commented on the manuscript before we submitted it. She did so remarkably promptly, and her comments were both encouraging and enlightening. She made us think through many points more carefully, and the book is a good deal better as a result of her work. At the same time, its remaining flaws cannot be laid at her door, but remain the responsibility of the authors.

The illustration in Chapter 3 of 'Sam's' differentiation between thoughts and feelings is drawn from D. Greenberger and C. A. Padsky, *Mind Over Mood*, New York, Guilford Press, 1995. It is reprinted with the kind permission of The Guilford Press.

We are grateful to the Movement for Reform Judaism for permission to quote lines from Judah Halevi's poem, 'Lord, where shall I find You?' (the poem is included in 'Meditations before prayer' in *Forms of Prayer for Jewish Worship I*, published by The Reform Synagogues of Great Britain), and to the General Secretary of the Anglican Church in New Zealand for permission to quote a prayer of absolution from *A New Zealand Prayer Book – He Karakia Mihinare o Aotearoa*, the new edition, published in 2005 by Genesis Publications, Christchurch, New Zealand.

Alison Barr, our editor at SPCK, and the whole SPCK team, have been encouraging of our endeavours throughout, from the time when first we discussed our ideas, through the initial trial pieces we submitted for consideration, right through to the final production of the book. We could not have wished for better.

Writing this book together has been an extremely stimulating and enjoyable exercise for us both, and we have learned and gained a huge amount from one another. But it would have been a different experience for us if our wives, Ken's Janis and Trevor's Caroline, had not been as unfailingly supportive and patient as they have been. Their love has kept us going, and to them we owe the largest debt. This book is dedicated to them.

1

'You're worth the effort': the basics

Let's imagine for one moment that life is very difficult, and you can't bring yourself to talk to your family or your friends about it, so you think you'll try a therapist. So you go on the internet, get into www.comparethetherapists.com (this is a fictitious address, so don't try it), choose one you like the sound of, and book an appointment. The day comes and you're feeling nervous. You're shown into the room, and the therapist gives you a warm handshake and a nice chair to sit on. But then the therapist says, 'Now there's one thing you should know before we begin. I've never made anyone better in my life.' 'Oh no!' you say to yourself. 'What a rubbish website! I knew this was a mistake.' You start to get up from the chair. 'Wait,' says the therapist. 'I don't mean I'm completely incompetent and you're wasting your time. The point is, we need to become a team, you and I. You're the one who is going to change your life. I can't do that for you. But I can offer you a helping hand. That's what I'm here for.'

And that's what this book is here for, to provide a helping hand for people who want to experiment with making changes in their lives against the shimmering, mysterious background of God's extraordinary, yet hard to grasp and hold, unconditional love.

It is not meant for those who have problems that are so intrusive that the service of a therapist is really needed. If your own distress fits one or more of the following descriptions, then you should think about supplementing the reading of this book by seeking the help of a psychological therapist, or seeing your GP.

- It impedes your performance at work, and has done so for a long time, or else prevents you from working altogether.
- It gets in the way of you doing things you see lots of other people doing, and would like to do yourself, such as the shopping, or having a good night's sleep.
- You don't like the way you react to others: you get angry with people, including those you live with; you avoid situations where other people are present.

This book uses the model of a particular approach to therapy designed for a wider audience, one indeed that we hope might be of benefit to all and sundry. It is for anyone who would like to enhance his or her practice of loving God by being effective in the equation, 'You shall love the Lord your God with all your heart, and with all your soul, and with all your strength, and with all your mind; and your neighbour as yourself.' Those are familiar words. They appear in Luke 10.27, with almost identical versions in Mark 12.30–31 and Matthew 22.37–39, and are often described as Jesus' summary of the Jewish law. Interestingly enough, Luke doesn't put the words in Jesus' mouth, but attributes them to an unnamed expert in the Jewish law. Jesus commends him by saying, 'You have given the right answer; do this, and you will live' (Luke 10.28). They come from two quite separate passages in the Hebrew Scriptures, in what we Christians generally call the Old Testament: Deuteronomy 6.5 and Leviticus 19.18.

For Paul, writing some time before any of the Gospels were composed, that second commandment from Leviticus, 'You shall love your neighbour as yourself', was enough by itself to sum up the whole law (see Galatians 5.14), while the author of the letter of James calls it 'the royal law' (James 2.8). It lies at the heart of Christian and Jewish living. The English version, 'Love your neighbour as yourself', is five words. The books of the New Testament were written in Greek, and when it is quoted there it amounts to six. But that is itself a translation, for Leviticus 19.18 was composed in Hebrew. The original is extremely terse, just three words, and has a certain ambiguity. Everett Fox, a contemporary Jewish scholar, in the translation of Leviticus in his book *The Five Books of Moses* has this: 'but be loving to your neighbour (as one) like yourself' (the brackets are his).[1]

However it is translated, it assumes we put a high value on ourselves, and that is what matters for the purpose of our argument. 'You are not to lie,' says that same chapter in Leviticus, 'You are not to hate your brother in your heart' (in verses 11 and 17, Fox's translation[2]), or in the earlier part of verse 18 itself, and again as Fox translates it, 'you are not to retain anger against the sons of your kinspeople.' Leviticus appears to suggest that we don't lie to ourselves about ourselves. But we do! It seems to assume we don't hate ourselves, or retain anger against ourselves. But we can, we do! And too often the Church doesn't help us. It is often very good indeed at challenging, inspiring and energizing us in the business of loving our neighbours. Countless Christians get on with that day in, day out in myriad circumstances. But it is not always so good at encouraging us to have a high opinion of ourselves, to love ourselves. This book is about giving people permission to love themselves – giving *you* permission to love yourself, to find for yourself the truth about those other famous words from the Old Testament about human beings being made 'in the image of God' (Genesis 1.26–27; the verses may be famous, but their true and startling significance is rarely understood, as we will explain later in this chapter).

Some of us were once taught to believe that loving God meant turning our backs on ourselves: 'the Cross crosses out the "I",' and all that. Somewhere the thought was put into our heads (certainly not by God himself) that if we put all our heart and soul and strength and mind into loving God, then there won't be any love left over for ourselves; indeed, that there *mustn't* be any love left over. Loving God means stopping loving ourselves. Perhaps it even means loathing ourselves.

And that, at times, can be surprisingly easy. We know ourselves too well. As Oliver Cromwell said, we know ourselves 'warts and all'; or else there are things about us we won't admit to. Together in our churches, for example, we may sing or recite the psalms, but we will carefully leave out those verses that pray for vengeance. And we will do that partly because we cannot face the truth about ourselves. As the great Old Testament scholar Walter Brueggemann writes:

> the yearning for vengeance is here, among us and within us and with power. It is not only there in the Psalms but it is here in the human heart and the human community. When we know ourselves as well as the Psalter knows us, we recognize that we are creatures who wish for vengeance and retaliation. We wish in every way we can to be right and, if not right, at least stronger.[3]

But God doesn't like that sort of thing. We've been taught that, too, over and over again. Which must mean that for a lot of the time God doesn't like *us*. Some have been taught that God actually hates them. Even in the UK some gays and lesbians have been told in plain terms that they are not welcome in church. In the USA they may have heard Jerry Falwell declare on television in March 1984 that homosexuals were 'brute beasts . . . part of a vile and satanic system [that] will be utterly annihilated, and there will be a celebration in heaven', or Jay Grimstead, Director of the Coalition on Revival, say with unblinking eye, 'Homosexuality makes God vomit.' Another American author wished to publish a book which covered areas far beyond sexuality under the title 'Ten reasons why God hates you'. His UK publisher (not the publisher of this book, we hasten to add!) had to persuade him that such a title might not be too good for sales.

Most Christians in the UK, thank God, have not come across preaching or teaching as vitriolic and toxic (and pathological) as that. But still some are carefully taught to be afraid of God. It is not too many years ago that one of us heard a nine-year-old girl say, with great confidence and conviction, 'God's up in heaven and he's on a throne and it's big and gold all over, and he sends people down, down, down to hell.' Please God she has shaken that god out of her soul, but it's more likely that he lurks still in the dark corners of her mind.

Nevertheless, the vast majority of us Christians are being told repeatedly that God loves us. He may not like us, but still, amazingly, he loves us. That's what we hear, but sometimes we are not convinced. 'It's all very well these people telling me how much God loves me despite what I am and do, but they don't know the me, the real me, inside, that makes me feel guilt and shame, that's been there all my life. Fundamentally I am, at best, deeply flawed, and there is nothing I can do about it.'

This last component of the belief is interesting. 'I am deeply flawed' is a statement about both the past and present; 'there is nothing I can do about it' is a statement about the future. Our past is our past, and we will look at it to try to understand and explain our present; but our past cannot be changed. What has happened to us and what we have done are facts of history; they are not available for modification, even when we think about the past very intensely, so hard it seems like reality. What we can do is change our evaluation of the past for the present and future. All of us can remember times when we have done something wrong in the past, and when we are reminded about it in the present we still feel pangs of guilt or shame. But we cannot undo what we have done; that is not available to us. But what is available with the passage of time is a rational reassessment of the events. Thus our self-judgemental statements can become less severe and condemnatory. The past is unchangeable, but the future is something else. Now surrendering our future to our past is something God really does not want us to do. That we both firmly believe.

Then there are all the other forces at large in our society that can undermine a proper valuing of ourselves: preoccupations with achievement (you have to *do something* to be worth anything), or with celebrity (you have to *be famous* to be worth something), or with status (you have to *be someone* to be worth anything). These are old lies, of course, but they are being told over and over again in our society with much conviction, and can exert much power over us. We know they're untrue, but still we believe them! And still they influence what we think and do.

But do not despair! Christianity is a religion of hope. There is something we can do, something *you* can do. In this book we will suggest experiments that you can work with, to see what helps and how much they work for you; then you decide if you want to use the changes made. As authors, we have an ethical responsibility here. The models and experiments we suggest are not plucked out of thin air, but are ones that years of clinical practice and pastoral experience suggest are both valid and effective. We are not about to tell you to do this or that, but are offering you an opportunity to experiment with alternative behaviour, thinking, and spiritual concepts and practice. We will make suggestions about how you can make small adaptations, perhaps a number of them in succession, and you can see how well they work for you and if you want to use them. There are a number of concepts that form the basics of the experiments we are going to suggest.

You're worth the effort

A famous cosmetics firm has a very clever advertising agency which came up with the simple catchphrase, 'You're worth it,' said by a glamorous model with a seductive whisper at the end of each TV advert for their products. The phrase caught on, but everyone knew it wasn't genuine; it was just being used to get us to buy or do something.

We want to change the phrase a little, to 'You're worth the effort.' And we *mean* it.

'We are made in the image of God.' We have heard or read those words many times. In truth they are far more radical than we generally think. They were probably written in the sixth century BC, during the time when so many of the people of Israel had been taken into exile in Mesopotamia by the Babylonians, and when they were face to face with the brutality and the swagger of Babylonian power. For longer than anyone could remember, the kings of Mesopotamia (and Egypt, also) had been proclaimed as being 'the image', or 'in the image' of a god. The remarkable poet who composed Genesis 1 stole those words from the palace in Babylon, and applied them to each and every human being, to women (as he carefully points out) as well as to men. In doing so he gave us one of the most radical political statements ever made: *all* human beings have royal status; *all of us* are kings and queens on God's wide earth! When someone puts a label on the back window of their car, encouraging us to drive carefully because they have a princess on board, they are right! They have! And who says so? God! The words of Genesis 1.26–27 are daringly political: indeed, for their times, treacherously so. But their meaning goes far beyond politics. They are one of the most beautiful, profound, pithy statements of the God-given worth of us human beings ever made.

The trouble is, the Church and its teachers soon lost sight of the original political background of the words, if they ever grasped it, needlessly complicated them and then distorted them. They started talking as if 'the image' and 'likeness' of God were something inside us, a part of us, and a part of us we sinful human beings had *lost*. A daring, exhilarating positive was turned into a damning negative, and, as we all know, negatives hit home. Some recent marketing research proposed that there was a ten to one ratio of recommendations to complaints when it comes to what influences our shopping behaviour. It seems we need to hear ten good things said about a product or store to get us to change our habits, but only one complaint. At a personal level we more readily hear and notice scolding than praise. We all know that, too.

How about adopting our 'You're worth the effort' as the catchphrase of this book, not for its feel-good factor, or as a theological concept, but rather because it works? Engaging with the experiments we propose here may need some courage, effort and determination, but they are worth the effort because *you* are worth the effort. Loving yourself is part of the equation. It will enable you to love your neighbour without giving him or her the hunted look. Loving yourself, truly loving yourself as God loves you, is not an egocentric and self-indulgent idea. Quite the reverse.

It ain't what you see, it's the way that you see it. Or, we are not distressed by things or events but by the way we perceive them.

A simple illustration, quickly followed by our first exercise.

Example 1

You are leaving church after the morning service. Your minister is a very affable person who not only sees it as a priority to welcome people but who also clearly enjoys it. Out of the corner of your eye you see Sam, who is new, shaking hands with the minister. But the minister is not her usual effusive self. A woman whose husband has recently died is clearly distracting her. She will be taking the funeral in a few days' time.

To resolve her dilemma the minister brings Sam over and introduces you. This is not uncommon. The church has a policy of sharing welcoming, and you have done this before. You start to have a conversation with Sam, but Sam is clearly not engaging with you. He looks almost anywhere other than you. He doesn't look you in the eye.

In the table on p. 9, we have listed three different thoughts you might have about this situation, and beneath each thought a range of moods it might provoke. Four moods are listed below each thought. Having decided which mood you think would follow each of the interpretations of Sam's not looking at you, make a note of it.

THOUGHT	'Sam is rude. He is discourteous and not taking any notice of me.'			
Possible moods	Irritated	Sad	Nervous	Caring
THOUGHT	'Sam doesn't find me interesting. I always knew I was boring.'			
Possible moods	Irritated	Sad	Nervous	Caring
THOUGHT	'Sam seems shy. He's probably too uncomfortable to look at me.'			
Possible moods	Irritated	Sad	Nervous	Caring

The situation remains the same. It is what we think, and how we interpret what is happening, that make a difference to how we feel. There also tends to be a relationship between the strength with which we hold the thought to be true and the intensity of the feeling. When railway trains were invented, some physicians debated whether the human body could withstand speeds of over 40 miles per hour. Queen Victoria heard about this view and forbade any train on which she was a passenger to exceed this speed. Sometimes the intensity of the feeling, in conjunction with the conviction that the thought is right, leads us to ignore evidence to the contrary. What if his family had constantly put Sam down, telling him he was of little worth and that people didn't want to know him? In those circumstances it's quite likely he would avoid looking at you and want to crawl into his hole. But suppose someone told you this about Sam after you had thought he didn't find you at all interesting, and that you bored everyone rigid, and when you were feeling extremely hurt as a result. Would the new information about Sam immediately change your thought and your feeling, or would you dismiss it as untrue?

Thoughts and feelings

We don't know how difficult you found that exercise but one aspect that seems to generate problems is the confusion, in modern speech, between thoughts and feelings. Idiomatically we frequently use the words as if they meant the same thing. For example, after a weather forecast promising mostly sunshine, we might say, 'I feel it's going to be a dry day.' However, there is no such emotion as 'it's going to be a dry day'; it's a thought. The context of that thought will influence how we feel. If we want to go for a picnic, then we may feel glad; if we are experiencing a drought and our garden is in serious need of water, we may feel some desperation. Or suppose as you are leaving church the vicar does not give her usual greeting but seems a bit distracted. We may walk down the path saying to ourselves, 'I feel the vicar doesn't like me', but 'doesn't like me' is a thought, not a feeling. If we have the thought 'the vicar doesn't like me', we may feel sad or rejected, or we may feel quite pleased because we have had a disagreement and upsetting her shows us we have won our point!

Example 2

Watch a TV play or film for no more than five minutes – it could be as little as 30 seconds. Choose a scene, and then consider the questions below. Make notes of your responses on a piece of paper, in columns under the headings shown below.

You should address column 1 first, and then columns 2 and 3 in the order that suits you. Try to differentiate carefully between contents of thoughts and of feelings, and then see how they relate to each other.

Column 1	Column 2	Column 3
What was going on? What was happening, who was saying/doing what to whom? Where was it? i.e. at home, in public, etc.	What were you thinking as you were watching the scene?	How were you feeling? Try to use emotion words like pleased, angry, disappointed, sad, etc.

We will often return to this concept of the difference between thought and feeling as the exercises progress.

The wholeness of you

A friend of ours recently had a very unpleasant experience. He had intense pain in the upper-right side of the abdomen, which doubled him up and was often accompanied by nausea and vomiting. He sought medical advice as soon as he could and was diagnosed with gallstones. He was admitted to hospital and was returned to health with an ease that seems extraordinary, given the evident distress and intensity of pain he had been experiencing. His treatment was keyhole surgery, a minimal intervention.

There is an interesting idea with regard to therapy of any description: its objective should be maximum benefit with minimum intrusion. And so we hope it will be with learning to love yourself. We are not seeking a big conversion experience, but rather straightforward and simple adjustments that can change direction and offer new horizons. Think of it like steering a boat or a car. Violent swings of the rudder of a boat put a big plate of wood or steel across the flow of water, slowing the boat down, and can make all on board uncomfortable. Similarly with a car, a sudden tight lock on the steering wheel puts the tyres across the direction of the car, can be dangerous as it will cause a skid, and is also uncomfortable. For both boat and car, slight, constant adjustments are more efficient and comfortable. In our experiments we will be suggesting only delicate adjustments.

If, then, we are not going for the spectacular, where do we focus the micro changes? We can think of ourselves like the diagram we call the Four Button Model (see Figure 1, overleaf). This model is very significant for our thinking in much of this book and we will refer to it on several occasions.

The surrounding oval is us; it is the wholeness of us. Psychologists or therapists call it a *gestalt*, where the whole is greater

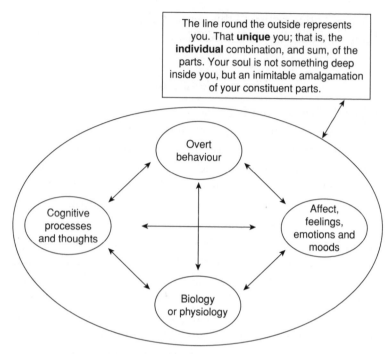

The line round the outside represents you. That **unique** you; that is, the **individual** combination, and sum, of the parts. Your soul is not something deep inside you, but an inimitable amalgamation of your constituent parts.

Overt behaviour

Cognitive processes and thoughts

Affect, feelings, emotions and moods

Biology or physiology

Figure 1 The Four Button Model

than the sum of the parts. While our thoughts, feeling, behaviour and biology are all components of us, it is the interaction between them that makes us what we are.

Let us give a simple if rather dramatic example. Ken once was therapist to a person who was an employee in an organization which was undergoing considerable stress. The source of the stress lay in events two decades past, but the repercussions in the form of police, regulatory and media investigation were very much in the present. The present was causing a significant cultural shock to people who had worked in the organization for many years and were now approaching the end of their careers; there was palpable fear about the present and future. The person who came to Ken because of his anxiety was finding it very hard and unpleasant to continue working. While talking about how he was managing his day at work, Ken discovered the person was drinking up to 15 cups of coffee each day during working hours. Coffee drinking is clearly a behavioural activity, but that much caffeine will have an effect on the neurological system (biology), releasing neurotransmitters associated with arousal and anxiety (feelings), and when we feel afraid, we scan and check for threats (thinking). So while there *was* a threat – the pressure the organization was experiencing – the man's excessive coffee drinking behaviour, and the associated chain of interactions in his system, made it considerably worse. It was relatively easy for him to change his behaviour, although the environmental factors operating on the organization remained beyond his control.

In this case there were various components. Let us examine them in a bit more detail.

Overt behaviour

Behaviour is what someone would see if they watched you very closely. It is overt. For example, they might see you opening and closing your house door, walking to the shop, buying some milk and walking home. But the close observer would also notice you clenching your fist and tightening your shoulders as you approached the road to cross over. They would have seen you tapping your feet and fiddling with your watchstrap as you waited to pay. They would not necessarily have put an interpretation on this behaviour, but they might have wondered if you'd noticed what you did.

Thoughts, memories, images and beliefs

This is thinking, 'I need to go and get some milk'; remembering, 'I get my milk at the shop across the road'; quickly choosing the carton of milk because you have an image of what it looks like – you don't need to read every label in the shop to find it. But we have memory images as well, and one of the possible reasons for clenching your fist and tightening your shoulders as you approached the road to cross over might be having witnessed someone being involved in a collision at that point and seeing the image again in your head. Sometimes our thoughts are very habitual and we are almost unaware of them; they are like an automatic mantra, many of them learnt when we were very young, and they influence how we see our world. They are like permanent glasses that so affect our perception that they become part of it. Some call these beliefs.

Feelings, emotions and moods

Feelings are important. Feeling unhappy and unworthy can make some people think that true love for others must go hand in hand with a lack of love or care for themselves. The belief that we are of no worth can also lead to feelings of inadequacy and to our avoiding others because, we say, 'Why would they want to know someone like me?' Feelings and emotions are therefore dependent on what we are thinking, but simultaneously influence thoughts. They are also very complex. Most parents can report mixed emotions about adolescent children who are developing their identity: concurrent and instantaneous feelings of love, frustration, bewilderment and anger. As we said earlier, it is important to develop the skill of differentiating between thoughts and feelings. In most cases feelings have particular adjectives or nouns attached to them such as angry, lonely, or love, enjoyment.

Biology and physiology

Imagine watching a film on the TV, at home on the comfort of your sofa, when suddenly there is a struggle between the two protagonists on the edge of a high cliff. You are so engaged in the plot, your stomach begins to churn and your palms dampen. In the Four Button Model this is the biological component. When watching an exciting film this is what we might expect. The person drinking all that coffee, however, had not made the connection between the environment he was working in, his caffeine coping strategy and his physiological response. He was feeling a sensation of physical discomfort without knowing why, and that only made him more anxious. The anxiety we can all recognize. What we are less aware of is the activity of the nervous system and its neurotransmitters. We will look at these in greater detail further on.

Example 3

We would like you to recall a few minutes before an occasion, preferably a good one, when you were very excited: when you were about to play your saxophone in your new jazz band's first gig; when you were about to go out on the pitch for a football match, or make a speech; when you were setting out to climb that mountain you'd been waiting to climb for years, or when you were about to meet one of your heroes; when you were going to try to resolve a difficulty in a problematic, but important relationship. Take a sheet of paper and write a brief summary of the event.

Now take a second sheet, and thinking of that exciting occasion, tackle the simple questions shown in the table below.

The rest of the book will use these basic concepts to help you try alternative ways of behaving and thinking. We will offer you an invitation to experiment with the following steps: first (and this has to be your starting point), to decide that you matter enough to try to make the change; second, to think about how you interpret the events in the world you live in and the behaviour of the people you meet as part of your everyday

Button	Your recall
Overt behaviour	When I remember .... my behaviour was ....
Thoughts	When I remember .... my thoughts were ....
Feelings/emotions	When I remember .... my feelings were ....
Physical sensations	When I remember .... my physical sensations were ....

life; third, to evaluate the strength of the evidence supporting that interpretation. After this, if you decide the evidence is not up to much, then we will invite you to consider alternatives that have greater strength and validity, or lead to an outcome you find more suitable for your life. Finally, we will look at how you can practise differentiating between thoughts, behaviours and emotions. That will be an important skill to develop, because thoughts and behaviours are more amenable to experimental change than emotions.

PEACE

Throughout the book we will follow the acronym PEACE. PEACE stands for Permission, Explanation, Acceptance and/or Adjustment, Coaching and Evaluation. Let us explain.

Permission

By 'permission' we mean giving ourselves permission to have the thoughts and feelings we are experiencing. It sounds simple, but sometimes it takes some effort and thinking about. If we say 'I should' or 'I ought' all the time, it is likely to make matters worse. To various degrees we become tense, ashamed or anxious, and that gets in the way of solving the problem we are facing.

You may be familiar with the concept of 'normal distribution'. Normal distribution is a representation of how characteristics are prevalent in living organisms. A commonly used example is people's height; the average height of a man in the UK is 1.77 m (or 69 in), but there are clearly some shorter and some taller than the average, and if you represent the range of heights on a graph you get what is known as a 'bell curve' (see Figure 2). For women, the UK average height is 1.62 m (or 64 in).

This bell curve applies to most differences among human beings, both physical and psychological. We can think of variations in shoe size and body temperature, or in the ability to do

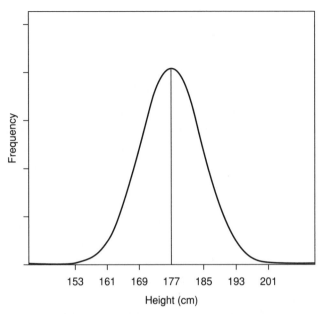

Figure 2 Normal distribution of average height for UK men

intelligence tests or remember things. It also applies to the usual range of human moods and emotions. Most of us will have a norm for our disposition and a range of moods either side of that norm. Much of the time we are just who we are. Our mood changes almost all the time, but in very small degrees. If it changes dramatically, however, and especially if that happens frequently, then problems can arise.

The way we respond to any event that happens to us reflects our memories, our perceptions, as well as our mental and spiritual state. If, for example, we are at the bus stop talking to Jenny, a woman we have never met before, how we conduct ourselves will be an amalgamation of our memories of similar encounters, our perceptions about people who look like Jenny, and our organic state at that moment.

The Four Button Model of a person (see Figure 1, p. 12) is of relevance here. There is significant evidence that mood levels from high to low correlate with levels of serotonin. Serotonin is one of the chemicals enabling information to be passed between nerve cells. When it is low, we do not feel good. When it is high, we feel more OK. The levels of serotonin vary from person to person and according to our situation. If we have had bad news, or we are disappointed, our serotonin levels drop. When we stroke our dog, our serotonin levels rise. All of this happens within the physiology button, but since each of the buttons is connected to the other three, the physiological event effects change in the others.

My behaviour towards Jenny will depend on a combination of factors. This definitely does not excuse being rude, bad-mannered, or overly familiar. Mature humans have insight into the possible consequences of their behaviour for other people, and can exercise a measure of self-control. But it does mean that if we get it wrong, we are not totally at fault and to be condemned. (If we do something that is wrong, we still need, of course, to acknowledge it, apologize and do what we can to make amends.)

So when we feel low, have a bout of the blues, are a bit depressed or even seriously depressed to the point we might be regarded as ill, it is not because we are bad people with an inherent weakness like the San Andreas Fault in the USA. It is because at that moment our perception of what is going on is causing us to respond in a manner we would like to be different.

Giving ourselves permission does not resolve the problem but it does normalize it. That does not mean it is desirable; quite the contrary, but it does open the possibility of change.

Explanation

We need to understand further how depression, anxiety, or low self-esteem originate and are maintained, to explore the behaviours and thinking styles that go with them, and to question their validity. Someone who is depressed, for example, characteristically thinks they are disliked, that indeed they are impossible to like, and that the future is hopeless. Is this true? Is it true of *us*? If it is not 'the truth, the whole truth and nothing but the truth', how can we behave and think differently if and when a similar situation occurs, so that we don't go down the next time to the same extent?

Acceptance and adjustment

Throughout the book we will refer to examples and experiments. Examples are exercises designed to help with understanding the points we are making. Experiments are exercises to help our readers make changes in their lives. These experiments will be to do with the judgements/assessments we make about our world and ourselves, and will explore different ways of behaving. People who have low mood, for example, often hide themselves away and reduce social contact. To do otherwise would require energy they feel they don't have – and why would other people want to know them anyway? If that is your situation, how can you break free?

Our exercises will establish a base line that will help you assess how much your distress is interfering with your life and ability to function. That in turn will allow you to judge how effective the exercises and experiments are.

Coaching

If the experiments in thinking and behaviour work, if they are effective in challenging unhelpful beliefs and assumptions and in moving you in the direction you want to go, then they need to be incorporated into your life and into your repertoire of responses to situations.

Evaluation

We will invite you to ask what works for you, and how you can try to protect yourself against unnecessarily bad consequences arising from your perception of distressing events in future.

Table 1.1 PEACE – the antidote to stress

P	Permission	• This means giving yourself permission to feel the way you do. • Given the circumstance, the way you are now could be logical, understandable, reasonable or even helpful. • That does not make it desirable, OK or functional. Nor does it mean that you are a victim of it. • The idea of permission is also about not giving yourself a hard time, beating yourself up or being fearful of what is happening.
E	Explanation and exploration	We have thought about how the way you are feeling is a response to how you are thinking and behaving; and how that in turn has been learnt from your experience of coping in the past. We can explore what thoughts influence and moderate these feelings, bad or good; they do not occur from nowhere: there is always a cause to produce the effect.
A	Acceptance and/or adjustment	This is very important. It is the changing of how you see things. It is having the discretion and humility to accept the things that we cannot change, the strength and courage to adjust the things we can change and the wisdom to know the difference between the two.
C	Coaching	This is the action point. It is doing experiments that enable the learning of new skills. It is using those skills to get the consequences you want for your life. It is about practising those skills to the stage where they become second nature before and during events that are problematic.
E	Evaluation	Evaluation is about experimenting with your new skills, finding out which work, and using them. Then giving yourself a 'well done' for being successful.

Table 1.1 sums up our explanation of PEACE. We will soon move on to the specific areas of depression, anxiety, worry and self-esteem, but first we need to say more about the experiments we will be proposing, and then add something on the subject of God.

2

'Don't trust me; I'm a doctor': the experiments

———◆·●·◆———

Frequently, as you read this book, we will be suggesting experiments for you to try. The purpose of this short chapter is to explain our emphasis on them and why they are so important.

A prominent clinical psychologist was heard on the radio to say, 'Don't trust me; I'm a doctor. Instead, trust the evidence from the experiments you make.'

Most of us from time to time try experiments; we order something from a menu we've never eaten before, to see what it tastes like. We travel to new places, to discover new scenery and meet different people. We read books by authors we don't know, to explore what they have to say and find out what we might learn from them. Most experiments like these either confirm or disconfirm our opinions or forebodings, perhaps our prejudices. Sometimes that is a joy, a true enlightenment; at other times it's a disappointment, while much of the time it falls between the two. Whatever the outcome, the experiment works *because it tells us something*.

Sometimes in conversation or the media we hear that an experiment 'failed' because the anticipated outcome, or the one hoped for, did not materialize. For example, a government may experiment with a new policy to achieve a particular change in society. If the change is not achieved, or not sufficiently so, the experiment is then said to have 'failed'. However, this is to misunderstand the purpose of experiments. The only experiments that fail are the ones that do not furnish us with any valuable information.

Suppose it is winter and there has been a hard frost. A pipe in the loft has frozen and our water supply is cut off. We experiment with heating the pipe. 'That should do it!' we say. We go outside, get some snow in a saucepan, boil it on the gas, climb up the loft ladder, somewhat gingerly, and pour the water over the pipe. As a result the pipe bursts and we still get no water – or rather, we do, only it's coming through the bedroom ceiling. 'Well, that experiment failed!' we say (among other things). Yet that is not true. Certainly the result is one we didn't want, and it does not solve the problem, either. We have learnt, however, that pouring very hot water on to frozen pipes can lead either to them fracturing, or to water pouring out of them when they have already been split by the expansion of the ice. The experiment can only properly be called a failure if we learn nothing by it, so that next time we have a frozen pipe, we do exactly the same thing with a pan of hot water and achieve the same result.

The experiments suggested in this book do not involve climbing loft ladders with pans of hot water, but they may or may not achieve the outcome you had hoped for. The difficulty here lies with us, the authors, not with you; we cannot know each of our readers individually. The components of the experiments we are suggesting are known to have effected change in many people, and to have brought them considerable and lasting benefit. They all have a firm basis in respected research and practice, but there is no research evidence to show that one particular component is applicable in all situations. If you try one of the experiments in this book, and it doesn't produce the change you had hoped for, do not say to yourself, 'Experiments don't work,' let alone, 'The experiment failed, and that means I'm beyond hope.' Say rather, 'Let's think about the experiment and see if there's something missing that could be included. Or perhaps we could redesign the experiment altogether.' The alternative is the status quo.

Christians cannot be content with the status quo. There is always room for hope and for change. And yet there may be some who are thinking, 'What's all this talk of experiments? What about grace and the work of the Holy Spirit? If I concentrate on what I can do, then I am denying God's work in my life and leaving him no room for manoeuvre.' But we aren't always required to leave things entirely in God's hands. Right at the start of the Bible, in Genesis 1, we human beings are assigned the great task of helping keep God's world in good order – and God persists with us, even when we make such a mess of things (the covenant with Noah in Genesis 9 and the call of Abraham in chapter 12 make that plain). God clearly wants us to work with him, so that he can look at the world once more and declare it 'very good'. Jesus called it building 'the kingdom of God'.

But even when we think we don't have the energy or confidence for that, or believe we couldn't possibly make a contribution of any value, God still calls us to act. Take, for example, the story of Jesus and the man with the withered hand in Mark 3.1–6, Matthew 12.9–14 and Luke 6.6–11. Jesus sees him one Sabbath when he goes to synagogue, and his attention is at once focused on him. In Mark's and Luke's versions Jesus asks him to do two things: 'Come forward,' he says to him, or, 'Come and stand here,' and then, 'Stretch out your hand.' He draws him out of the shadows and challenges him to take centre stage. That in itself is hard for the man to do. No doubt he prefers not to be noticed, at least when he's not begging, and he hasn't come to synagogue to beg. But Jesus' second challenge is surely impossible for him: 'Stretch out your hand.' He can't do that! His hand has no life in it; the muscles are completely wasted! If he tries to stretch it out, everyone will see how useless it is and how useless *he* is! Nevertheless, he does what is asked of him. He gets up, comes into the middle, and stretches out his hand. He could have slunk out of the synagogue with his still shrunken hand. But he doesn't. He experiments. How does he find the strength and courage to do that? Because in the presence of Jesus he knows he is *not* useless. Jesus empowers him at the start, when he sets him centre stage. He accords him a worth he has never known or felt before, and which no one has ever given him – that comes out especially in Matthew's version. That new sense of worth flows through him and into his hand. He *can* stretch it out! His life is changed.

We are not always required simply to 'wait upon the Lord'. We are called to be actively engaged in taking God's plans forward. Those plans are not for us to be depressed instead of having hope, or to be anxious, worried and fearful instead of being confident, or to think of ourselves as worthless rather than as God's treasured companions. God's plan is for us to have life in all its fullness, and if we have to make an effort to get there, then that is evidence of his care and of the dignity he affords us. We have to experiment, get out of our comfort zone, and like that man in the synagogue stand beside God.

Think of the great experimental scientists of the Enlightenment. For many of them, such as Newton or Hooke, their experiments revealed the wonders of God's creation. If we are not experiencing the abundant life God intends for us, then we also may need to experiment.

Remember, the only failed experiments are the ones that don't tell you anything. So you don't need to be afraid of them.

But it may take more than one attempt.

3

A bit more about God

In our opening chapter we introduced the subject of what we may, or may not, have been taught about God. It is worth revisiting that discussion and going deeper, before we proceed with the subjects of depression, anxiety, worry and self-esteem. For how you react to what we say there, and particularly to the experiments we propose, will be influenced by what you have come to believe, or disbelieve, about God.

In that first chapter we quoted a nine-year-old girl: 'God's up in heaven and he's on a throne and it's big and gold all over, and he sends people down, down, down to hell.' Someone had taught her to talk like that. She was not expressing her own spirituality, or her own encounters with God. That was obvious from the way she spoke, from the look in her eye and her body language. Trevor was sitting with a small group of children in Chester Cathedral, and he'd asked them, 'What comes into your head, when I say the word "God"?' The girl had replied immediately, without a moment's hesitation. Trevor has never forgotten her words. They were at once seared upon his brain and will remain there. That girl will now be a young woman. One might hope she has found a quite different God by now, or rather that a quite different God has found her. But we suspect that God will have had a job on his hands, for she seemed to have been taught too well.

Let us examine her words more closely. They are false on every single count! God is not 'up in heaven'. Yes, God is Other, yes, God is Beyond, is Mystery-beyond-mystery, yes, as Trevor once had God say:

25

> I bear whole galaxies in the hands you pierced;
> the light and dark of space are held in their entirety
> within the pupils of my eyes;
> the universe itself is the smile upon my face.[4]

But we Christians have a remarkable claim to make about this God: he is *down here, in our midst, in the here and now*. That is what we mean by a God incarnate. We don't mean that once God came down to earth 2,000 years ago, and after an all too short spell went back to heaven again. That is how the story is sometimes told, but the truth revealed by Jesus of Nazareth is that God is with us, always was, always will be. We can *touch* the Beyond! The Other is familiar! The Mystery remains a mystery, but nevertheless has been revealed!

And this God among us is not on any 'throne' either, let alone one that is 'big and gold all over'. The Man-who-shows-us-God, Jesus of Nazareth: when in the Gospels does he walk the corridors of power? Once and only once, when he is in Pilate's headquarters and on his way to crucifixion, that most disgusting of all Roman forms of execution, reserved for those they regarded as the lowest of the low, slaves and what we would today call terrorists. (Yet his crucifixion, all the Gospels agree, is the moment when the mystery of God is most clearly revealed.)

And before his death, so John tells us, he washed the feet of his friends. That was a most extraordinary thing to do. Most people, Jesus included, washed their own feet, whenever they crossed the threshold of their own or someone else's house. Only the rich had slaves to wash them for them, and the particular slaves given that job were young girls, the 'tweenies' of their day, right at the very bottom of the households' pecking order.

> Do not look up to find your God
> enthroned above the circle of the earth;
> look down to find him at your feet
> with towel tied round about his waist.[5]

And this most extraordinary God most certainly does not send 'people down, down, down to hell'. For 2,000 years powerful men in the Church have sometimes been trying, for their own ends, to put the fear of God into children like that nine-year-old girl in the Cathedral, and into adults, also, when they should have been putting the love of God into them instead. To put the fear of God into children is not only a blasphemy, it is a form of abuse. It is still going on.

The greatest of Jesus' parables is found in Luke 15.11–32. Often called the Parable of the Prodigal Son, it is better called the Parable of the Two Brothers. For many of us the figure of the father in the story presents us with an image of God, and leaves us with some astonishing pictures to hold in our minds.

When the younger son returns home, 'while he was still far off', the parable goes, 'his father saw him and was filled with compassion; he ran and put his arms around him and kissed him.' Then the father says to his slaves, 'Quickly, bring out a robe – the best one – and put it on him; put a ring on his finger and sandals on his feet. And get the fatted calf and kill it, and let us eat and celebrate; for this son of mine was dead and is alive again; he was lost and is found!' Why does the father run up the road, when in those days men in his position simply did not run like that? Why does he care nothing for his precious honour in the village, but instead behaves as a mother might (for a mother was free to run)? Why does he seem to pay no heed to the fact that his son had so humiliated him when he'd asked for his inheritance, and had threatened the family with ruin when he went off with it all and blew the lot? The answer to these questions is quite plain: because of his compassion (Luke says so, in 15.20, which we have quoted already – 'Just look at the state of him!' we hear the father saying), and because his son is alive and back home, and *that is all that matters*.

But the parable is only at its mid-point. In the second half the elder son appears. The great feast for his brother is in full swing, but he refuses to go in. Jesus' hearers would have been shocked by that. 'The elder son *must* go in,' they would have said. 'He must put his own feelings aside, go and embrace his brother, and help his father entertain the guests. That's his clear duty.' His refusal to go in is humiliating for his father. They would have thought that, too. 'No doubt, the father will send a slave outside to tell the brother to come in and do his duty.' But no, not in this parable: 'His father came out and began to plead with him,' and when as a result he gets the full force of his son's anger hurled in his face, he replies, 'My child' (most translations have 'son', but Luke's Greek has 'child', a more tender and intimate term), 'you are always with me, and all that is mine is yours.'

Has this father still no regard for his position in the family? No, he hasn't. In coming out to plead with his son, is he not behaving again like a mother, and is not 'child' mother talk? Yes, he is, and yes, it is. The father of this parable is a fool. That's how Jesus' hearers would have seen him, and many contemporary New Testament scholars agree with them. Some feel it so strongly that they say he cannot therefore give us an image of God. But did not Paul say in 1 Corinthians 1.25, in one of the most profound verses in his letters, 'God's foolishness is wiser than human wisdom, and God's weakness is stronger than human strength'? Paul is commenting on the crucifixion there; he could just as easily be speaking of the Parable of the Two Brothers.

So God's compassion, God's love for us, turns him into a fool! God cares nothing for his own honour or authority; he cares nothing for being God! He cares only for us, and the rest of his creation. God is never preoccupied with himself. He is always turned outwards towards his creatures, and when he sees us, he cries, 'Look at the state of him! Look at the state of her!' and he runs up the road to meet us and fling his arms about us, and we find ourselves wiping the tears of God from our cheeks.

Such a vision is not found only among Christians. That is hardly surprising, for if God is really like that, some of other faiths who have met him will inevitably speak of him as we do. 'If you take two steps towards God, God runs to you!' Those words are put into the mouth of a Muslim character by Yann Martel, in his novel *Life of Pi*. And Judah Halevi, a Jewish poet and philosopher who lived in Spain and then Palestine between 1075 and 1141, wrote:

> I have sought Your nearness,
> With all my heart I called You
> And going out to meet You
> I found You coming to meet me.[6]

Some years ago Trevor preached a story-sermon in Chester Cathedral which he called 'The hands of God'. A prison chaplain was one of the visitors in the congregation that Sunday, and after the service she asked for a copy of it, because it brought to her mind so many of the men she knew in the prison where she worked. The hero of the story is a man who has been in and out of prison all his life, and has never had any time for God. He dies alone, and someone from social services is the only person at his funeral.

'I thought it was all because I was abused as a child,' he explains,

> but I didn't expect God to agree with that. After all, he knows just how bad we really are, doesn't he. My old Dad taught me that when I was a kid, when he got his strap out, and my Mum said the same when she did those other things with me. I was a bad boy, they said, a bad, bad boy. I believed them, of course. Well, you do, don't you. I never gave up believing them. I died still believing them.

So when he finds himself after death in the presence of God, he is more than a bit surprised. He had thought he would find himself 'in the other place, down among the teeth-gnashers'.

Yet this is only the start of it. His biggest surprise is when he finds 'God's house' down a side street.

God's house.

Now that was a disappointment, at least at first. If you'd asked me what God's house was like, I'd have said it must be enormous and really grand and gold all over, with windows too high up to see into and flights of tall steps and angels guarding the doors, huge doors, banged up shut and too heavy for anyone ordinary to open, so the angels would have to open them for you, only they would only do that if you'd been very good all your life, and I hadn't, so that was that as far as I was concerned, and anyway the place was far too posh, and too frightening an' all, if I was honest, which I rarely was.

But this wasn't like that at all! It was small and ordinary, and the windows were low down, and the door was open and there were angels inside with one of them playing jazz on a piano with the front off and a load of people having the best time of their lives by the sound of it and I didn't know if they would let me in when one of the angels came out and brought me inside and I stood there feeling a bit of a lemon and my angel had disappeared into the kitchen and I couldn't see God anywhere and I was just going to go back out again when she came out to see me. Just to see *me*! Deliberately! My God was in the middle of making bread, and was up to her elbows in flour, and she came out on purpose, at a tricky stage of the operations, just to see me! I didn't know God wore a pinny! And all of a sudden I remembered my Mum, and I nearly turned and ran. But she came right up to me and gave me a great big hug, like no hug I'd ever had before. I mean it was for me, not just for her. And then she went back to her baking.

I've never been the same since, of course. I'm getting quite good at the jazz, and the baking, with God. And I still have the marks of God's floury hands on my back. Everyone does up here.[7]

That is the kind of God the two of us have found, or rather the kind of God that has found us. We too have the marks of God's floury hands on our backs. Maybe you can begin to imagine them on your own back, or catch sight of God running up the road to meet you, or hear him saying to you, 'all that is mine is yours,' or you can look down to see him kneeling to wash your feet.

Think not of what you may have been taught *about* God. Think instead of your own encounters with God, those moments when you discovered the Reality at the heart of reality, those moments that were both the most exhilarating and the most challenging of your life. Think of those moments when you 'took off your shoes'.

> Earth's crammed with heaven,
> And every common bush afire with God:
> But only he who sees, takes off his shoes;
> The rest sit around it, and pluck blackberries.
> (Elizabeth Barrett Browning, *Aurora Leigh*)

Most of the time we just pluck blackberries, but sometimes we see, we find the holy, and remove our shoes.

And remember, God can never, ever be worse than the best we can imagine or experience among human beings. Far too often religious people, including Christians, make God out to be worse than us. Think again of those who'd taught that young girl Trevor met in Chester Cathedral. But God cannot be less forgiving, less generous, less loving than the most forgiving, the most generous, the most loving of human beings. That is a divine impossibility! We have all come across or heard about people whose persistent love, generosity, or forgiveness make our jaws drop and provide us with lasting inspiration. If that's what people are capable of, then what in heaven's name is God like?

To that we Christians might reply, 'Stand at the foot of the cross and see!'

4

'And there is no health in us': depression

God's forgiveness comes first

If we had had the facility we would have started this chapter with a recording of 'Every time we say goodbye' by Ella Fitzgerald or a song by Bessie Smith or Billie Holiday. Those artists were among the best singers of the blues the world has ever seen. So as a preparation, if you have a recording of any of them, you might care to listen to it first to get you into the mood. Alternatively, it can all be found on YouTube. All three of these singers knew what was meant by the blues, especially Billie and Bessie. They had an experience of life that was hammered on a very hard anvil.

We are talking in this chapter about a range of emotions, from fed up to feelings of depression, that interfere with our ability to live our lives in a way we would like. We hear from our Bibles, 'You shall love your neighbour as yourself', but sometimes loving ourselves is hard work, and we end up feeling, in various degrees, useless, worthless and generally out of sorts.

The chapter's title is a sentence taken from the General Confession of Morning or Evening Prayer in the Book of Common Prayer. It follows some other words, 'We have offended against thy holy laws. We have left undone those things which we ought to have done; And we have done those things which we ought not to have done,' and it proceeds to require those using the confession to describe themselves as 'miserable offenders'. This is florid seventeenth-century language, and the word 'miserable' here means wretched, in need of mercy or pity. Yet still that prayer of confession rubs it in: we are very wicked, it seems, and the first thing we have to do in our approach to God is to tell him so and beg for his forgiveness. In the Book of Common Prayer even the so-called 'Absolution' that follows the Confession does not quite do what it says on the tin. It tells us that God 'pardoneth and absolveth all them that truly repent, and unfeignedly believe his holy Gospel'. And it continues, 'Wherefore let us beseech him to grant us true repentance, and his Holy Spirit, that those things may please him, which we do at this present; and that the rest of our life hereafter may be pure, and holy; so that at the last we may come to his eternal joy ...'

There is no unconditional forgiveness here. God's acceptance is limited to those who repent first, and to those who 'unfeignedly believe his holy Gospel'. That immediately cuts out most of the population of this country, indeed the world, and if we feel our own faith is shaky, as we might in time of trouble, we ourselves will feel excluded.

Contemporary orders of service tend to express greater confidence in God's forgiveness. Think, for example, of the wonderfully succinct prayer of absolution in the Prayer Book of the Anglican Church in New Zealand: 'God forgives you. Forgive others; forgive yourself.'[8] That prayer gets us far nearer the heart of the Christian faith and it acknowledges a great truth of human experience: when we encounter the forgiveness of God, whether through direct encounter with him or mediated through the acceptance of others, then we find we can forgive those who have hurt us and come to terms with who we are. Yet still, in the book of the New Zealand Church, those fine words are pronounced only after the prayer of confession; even there repentance comes first. In modern Christian worship, outside the Quakers, one of the first things we are generally required to do is confess our sins. The presumption seems to be that we are seriously unworthy of God's presence, and that first we must clear the decks before we can get on with the rest.

The Gospels tell a different tale: the story of a God who runs up the road to meet us when we have done dreadful things and are in a fearful state, runs as only a mother might; a God who runs as fast as she can out of sheer compassion; who runs not to condemn, but to embrace and to shower with honours. Or the story of a God who searches for us in the dark, as a shepherd might look for a lost sheep, found missing when the rest of the flock is gathered at the end of the day; of a God who lights her small oil lamp, goes down on her hands and knees, runs her fingers through the dirt and the muck of the floor, until she has us once more, her precious silver coin, held tight in her hand. Story after story in the Gospels tells of people who encountered Jesus and discovered they had a worth and a dignity that no one had accorded them before, and which they themselves had never entertained in their wildest dreams. They were members of the family of God, no less, able to call him 'Abba': his sons and daughters, sitting at his table, while he, the God of the universe, waited upon them, and even knelt to wash their feet. Discovering that, they could repent whole-heartedly, and get on with the job of building the kingdom of God without their sins getting so much in the way. Once they repented, they could enjoy Jesus' and God's forgiveness to the full. But in each and every case forgiveness and warm embrace came first.

The truth is, we have a loving Father 'whose nature is to have mercy', who forgives us before we confess, and who simply can do no other than love us unconditionally. But we also know that our thoughts and feelings change. One time we will be on top of the world, assured, cheerful and sensing a ready access to God's grace. At others we may be much less resilient; we may be getting over a bout of flu, or recovering from an operation. Our husband or wife may have died, and everyone is telling us we should have got over it by now, but it isn't the same cooking for one, the bed is empty and cold, and the larger emptiness inside us won't go away. We may have lost our job, or are having a really difficult time at work. Or we may have made a mistake or done something wrong, and are cross and fed up with ourselves, or deeply ashamed. This can be like a blanket of cloud, which the sunshine of forgiveness has difficulty in penetrating. That phrase 'miserable offenders' comes back to haunt us, and we remain convinced that 'miserable' means not in need of mercy, but deserving of condemnation.

Is God to be praised, no matter what?

Of course, relatively few Christians, even if they belong to the Church of England, remain familiar with the Book of Common Prayer. Yet even if you are used to a much less formal style of worship, you may still have noticed that many extemporary prayers share a significantly disproportionate emphasis on the worthlessness of those who pray. The language used, far from telling us how precious we are as children of our heavenly Father, rubs it in that we are permanently contaminated and useless. We are left feeling low and dejected.

It only makes matters worse if we are also being told that Christian faith goes hand in hand with joy, and that God is always to be praised and thanked, no matter what. 'It is indeed right,' we might hear the priest saying, 'it is our *duty* and our joy, *at all times and in all places* to give you thanks and praise.'[9] Notice the words we have put in italics. They are not true, but they are recited as if they were, as if thanks and praise of God were compulsory. And the hymns and songs we often sing together reinforce that impression. Though the prayer of lament and complaint is so common and so powerful in our Bibles, we only have 'Songs of Praise' on the television or in our local church, never 'Songs of Lament', let alone 'Songs of Complaint'. Many contemporary songs or hymns are published by Thankyou Music. We've yet to come across any desperate hymns from a publisher called Godhelpme! Music, let alone any angry and bitter ones from MyGodmyGodwhyhaveyouforsakenme? Music.

Imagine you are going through a really low patch, and finally you have found the courage and the energy to return to church, and the minister announces in an impossibly cheerful voice that everyone will stand and sing:

> Oh, I feel like dancing,
> it's foolishness, I know;
> but when the world has seen the light,
> they will dance with joy
> like we're dancing now.[10]

No doubt the person who wrote those lines did not mean to make anyone feel excluded, but surely, if dancing for joy is the last thing you could possibly think of doing, then you will feel you don't belong. After all, doesn't it say the world will dance with joy when they see the light? By that token, we say to ourselves, if I can't dance with joy, then I must have lost the light; I must have lost God, and God must have lost me. I'm an outsider. Just when I most need God's welcome, I'm denied it! Just when I most need to feel I belong, I'm made to feel an outcast! It's bad enough being depressed!

All church ministers know of people who have deliberately stayed away from church when they were going through difficult times. Can you blame such people, if the Church has put it across that its worship is for people who feel all right, people who feel like dancing for joy? Best stay indoors. Going out and joining other people is hard enough in any case.

The darkness in the Bible

Yet, if we do feel dejected, even if we have been battling depression for years, then there are significant works in the Bible that are on our side and may give eloquent expression to how we see ourselves and the world around us.

Almost all the psalms in the Old Testament touch upon the darker side of human experience, whether it be the experience of the individual or the community. Indeed the only psalm that is full of light, without shadows of any kind, is Psalm 150. And the darkest one of all is Psalm 88:

> My soul is full of troubles . . .
>> I am like those who have no help . . .
> like those whom you remember no more,
>> for they are cut off from your hand.
> You have put me in the depths of the Pit,
>> in the regions dark and deep.
> Your wrath lies heavy upon me,
>> and you overwhelm me with all your waves.
>
> You have caused my companions to shun me;
>> you have made me a thing of horror to them.
> I am shut in so that I cannot escape . . .
>
> O Lord, why do you cast me off?
>> Why do you hide your face from me? . . .
>> I am desperate . . .
> You have caused friend and neighbour to shun me;
>> my companions are in darkness.

'Darkness' is the last word of the psalm, and lest you think that this is an accident of translation, when we turn to the original Hebrew, we find the final word is indeed 'mahshak': 'in darkness', or 'in a dark place'.

Psalm 88 is stunning poetry, summing up in a few words, almost too beautiful to bear their meaning, the isolation of those who are in despair, who feel cut off from others, including those who love them, and cut off also from God; those who feel beyond any help, whether human or divine. And if we feel like that, we may conclude it is all God's fault. The poet of Psalm 88 does. That poem is a prayer of lament and complaint prayed in the pitch dark, when there is no light at the end of the tunnel. Nor does it emerge into the light; it ends still in a dark place, in total darkness.

And yet it is prayed! There is an energy about its lines, which often is denied us when we feel especially low, or when we have sunk (notice the metaphor) into depression. Those who pray Psalm 88 and the other dark psalms look God in the eye and tell him how it is. They demand to be heard. They accuse God of letting them down, and call upon him to come to their aid.

In the book of Ecclesiastes, that fight and that energy are missing. 'Vanity of vanities, says the Teacher, vanity of vanities! All is vanity.' That is how the book begins in 1.2, and how it ends in 12.8. The word for 'vanity' in the Hebrew means 'emptiness', 'futility', or 'absurdity'. James Crenshaw, who published a commentary on Ecclesiastes in 1988, translates it as, 'Utter futility! Utter futility! Everything is futile!', or 'Absurdity of absurdities . . . everything is absurd.'[11]

Most Christians don't know Ecclesiastes very well. But there is one famous passage, which begins in 3.1–2: 'For everything there is a season, and a time for every matter under heaven: a time to be born, and a time to die; a time to plant, and a time to pluck up what is planted . . .' The beguiling rhythms and sentiments of that passage have made it a choice for many a wedding service or funeral, and when it is read the reader invariably stops at 3.8. In the following verses, however, the Teacher spoils it all. 'What gain have the workers from their toil?' he asks, and then he denies that we human beings can find any pattern in things; although, indeed, there is a right time for everything, we cannot be sure what that is and often get it wrong. God, he says, keeps us in the dark, and there is no way of breaking out of our ignorance. God is not often mentioned in Ecclesiastes, but when he is, he appears remote, unknowable and frightening – you never know what he might do next. The final chapter of the book is given over to a poem about old age, which is thoroughly depressing: the body and its faculties fall apart, the eyes don't work properly any more, and just going out of the house becomes a frightening prospect. 'Utter futility!' the author cries. 'Everything is futile!'

When we are feeling low, all this might seem the last thing we wish to hear. Yet wait. The book of Ecclesiastes, with its eloquent expression of what we might now call depression, is found in our Scriptures! Very few books made it into the Bible. The whole of it, let alone the Old Testament by itself, is shorter than *War and Peace*, and it's a tiny volume when compared to *Encyclopaedia Britannica*. It's a very select body of writings. In the case of the Hebrew Bible, the Old Testament as we Christians call it, the few books that are included were those the Jews considered their very greatest treasures, and the ones that had stood the test of time. But *Ecclesiastes*?! Why in heaven's name did they choose *that*? For two main reasons, perhaps: the great beauty of the writing, and its boldness in speaking the truth. You only have to begin reading Ecclesiastes in the Hebrew to realize that you are in the presence of a great lyric poet. The Hebrew of those opening lines in 1.2, for example, is exquisite. But surely the main reason why the book was carefully handed on from one generation to the next and eventually placed in the same collection as Genesis, Isaiah, the Psalms and the story of Ruth, is that it spoke plainly about an all too common feature of human experience. For countless people it rang true, and it put into words, fine memorable words, exactly what they were feeling, if not all the time, then in dark days, weeks or months.

But that's the Old Testament, some Christians would say. When we get to the New, we find the good news, indeed the Good News to end all good news. 'Look,' they say, 'we even call our Bible the *Good News Bible*.' And yet at the heart of the New Testament, and as part of the climax of each of its four Gospels, we find a fearful tale of crucifixion and a God in the dark. It is told with utmost restraint, but with unflinching gaze. This point in the story of Jesus of Nazareth is the moment when God comes out into the open. The curtain of the temple, that once imprisoned God in the cramped, incense-filled cell of the Holy of Holies, is ripped apart and God walks free – except he cannot walk, because his hands and feet are pinned to Roman wood. He *will* walk free, of course, when in the dark, before dawn, before anyone gets there, he slips out of the tomb. But he will walk with a limp, the dreadful scars of his execution still upon him.

Each of the Gospel writers has told the crucifixion story in their own way, but Mark, Matthew and Luke all speak of the whole land being plunged into darkness between noon and three in the afternoon. What should have been the brightest part of the day was turned into pitch black. And in the midst of that dark was God, his arms stretched wide for embrace. The book of Ecclesiastes, with its devastating, treasured honesty, can say to those who are themselves depressed, 'I know. I've been there too. This also belongs to being human. You are not alone, not as isolated as you think. And you do not have to pretend. How you are does not amount to a lack of faith, even if it feels like it. You still belong to the family of God. Look at me, I'm in the Bible!' Yet the Gospels, with their tales of a crucifixion on one black Friday, go far beyond that. They reach out in the dark . . . and find the hand of God!

But what if we don't? What if we stretch out our hand, and find nothing? Then we need to find other ways of restoring and maintaining the balance.

Let's do it through PEACE.

Permission

A very influential psychiatrist called Aaron Beck characterizes our thinking when we are feeling depressed as having a combination of three beliefs.

1 **We think negatively about ourselves.** We have a raft of thoughts, which we believe to be true, that denigrate us. For example, we think of ourselves as unlikeable by 'normal' others, even those close to us. We sometimes create elaborate ruses to justify our belief. We say to ourselves, 'They wouldn't say how much they dislike me, they're too polite, but I know if

they knew what I was really like, they'd be appalled.' Typified by 'I'm worthless.'

2 **We think that the world, and our bit in particular, is a hostile, at best an unfriendly place that regards us with contempt.** It is unfair because those who are worthy are denied, or castigated, and the unworthy get the cream. To survive you have to be motivated by anger and constantly vigilant. Typified by 'Everybody hates me because I'm worthless.'

3 **We see the future, especially ours, as hopeless and pointless.** All attempts to influence our futures are pointless. The black holes in our persona fatally contaminate any attempt to make our lives any different. Typified by 'I'll never be good because everybody hates me because I'm worthless.'

Beck describes this as the Cognitive Triad of Depression. It is a vicious circle of inexorable and negative logic: 'I'm worthless' results in 'everybody hates me because I'm worthless', which results in, 'I'll never be good because everybody hates me. So I was right, I'm worthless.' We may even wonder whether God thinks this of us as well. Underneath, and energizing all of this, is fear.

If this triad gets momentum and persists for some time, it can produce symptoms that are typical of what is called depression. This is not a clinical textbook so we will refrain from listing all the symptoms clinicians use. However, the triad is sometimes accompanied by some of the following features:

- disrupted patterns of sleep, or sleep that is not refreshing (either too much or too little), which leads in turn to fatigue or loss of energy
- irritability
- sadness
- loss of interest, or pleasure, in activities
- changes in diet.

Let's start by considering the triad. In each of the parts of the triad, 1–3 above, there are statements in quotation marks: for example, 'I'm worthless'. The quotation marks are deliberate because they indicate examples of what we may say to ourselves in our heads, what some call 'self-talk' or 'self-speak'. Most of us talk to ourselves in our heads a lot of the time; it is a significant component of our thinking. If we are following directions, we may repeat them to ourselves as we walk or drive along, 'First on the right, past the Rose and Crown, second left ...' and so on. This self-speak may not just act as an aide-memoire, but on some occasions may also express what we think about ourselves and can be a reaction to particular situations. Dropping a cup and breaking it, for example, may result in us giving ourselves a hard time about being ham-fisted. 'You clumsy butter-fingered fool!' (or worse ****), may be our self-speak response. On the other hand, if we see something we've been involved in working out really well, we may be too modest to say it out loud, but our self-speak may go along the lines of, 'You did well there; that's good.' Whether we are aware of our self-speak or not, most of us do it all the time. It's a mechanism whereby we live reflectively and give meaning to our own and other people's behaviour.

It is appropriate to give attention to two aspects of our self-speak: its contents and origins.

When we are giving ourselves a hard time the nature of the self-speak we use is often imperative, absolute and judgemental (but frequently lacking in evidence). It is imperative because it contains lots of musts, shoulds and oughts. Underneath 'I am worthless' is often a subtext, 'Everyone knows I'm worthless, but I *should/must* be valued and useful, like everyone else. But every time I try I fail, so I really am worthless.' That is, to be of worth I *must* be seen by others to succeed in everything I do!

This unhelpful self-speak is absolute because it has no grada-tion. It's on/off, black/white, light/pitch dark, everything/nothing, everybody/nobody, always/never. So from triad 2 we have, 'Everybody hates me because I'm worthless' – not, 'Some people don't like me, but nobody is liked by everyone and, anyway, not being liked is not the same as being hated.' It's absolute: one person equals everyone. When we are feeling low we may not say out loud, 'They hate me,' but our negative emotions and self-speak are so absolute, they contaminate our perception. Even acts of kindness by others can be seen as expressions of contempt and hatred.

Our self-speak is judgemental because it negatively prejudges our outcomes and futures; no matter what we do, failure is the only outcome because we are of no worth. As triad 3 says, 'My future is bleak because I'll never be good because everybody hates me because I'm worthless.' Note the three 'becauses'; it's a spiral, or vicious circle, of ruthless consequential logic or connections. Our tendency to fall into it is a result of the inter-action between our low mood and our low thoughts and our low behaviour – with not a shred of evidence to support it.

This kind of imperative, absolute and judgemental self-speak, which lowers our mood and inhibits our potential, is frequently repetitive and habitual. It can be like an MP3 file in our heads that just gets switched on by certain select, activat-ing events. The activating events are unique to each of us, but because the self-speak is so habitual and automatic, it doesn't allow time for consideration of the distinctive features of each activating event. Our blaming ourselves for dropping the cup takes no account of the cup's value, or of the particular circumstances. Was it an old, chipped piece of crockery we were thinking of throwing out, or an item from a hitherto complete eighteenth-century Wedgwood dinner set? Was it passed to us by someone else during the washing up, wet and slippery? Were our hands stiff and numb from cold? When we are distressed, or tired, we tend to ignore questions like that and make it all personal and self-accusing.

So how did we come by this thinking style that prevents us from loving ourselves? We learnt it. We were certainly not born with it. A story from our childhood illustrates what we mean. Both of us authors started school in the late 1940s when Ofsted was not even a gleam in an Education Secretary's eye. Inspection in those days was by representatives of the great and the good. One visit in particular left its mark on the memory. Because of the war's disruption to family life it was quite common for six year olds to have brothers in their early twenties, and so it was with Tom. His elder brother had just had a child. But Tom (Ken cannot remember his name but the event remains) was from what would now be called a socially challenging family. The teacher, wanting to give him something to feel special about, asked him to stand up for the inspector and said, 'Tom, what are you?' She was hoping he would reply, with obvious pride in his voice, 'An uncle, Miss.' But there was silence while Tom thought. Then, with his head bowed, he murmured, 'A naughty boy, Miss.' Where did that come from, and is Tom, even 60-odd years later, still believing it? We don't know, but on that day, in that situation, it was the self-speak that came into Tom's head.

The Church has sometimes colluded in encouraging such negative self-speak, and still does. Too often God is cast as a distant king and judge, looking down on us in more ways than one, watching our every move, ready to pounce and punish when we put a foot wrong. A friend of Trevor's recently visited a parish church for the Sunday service, where the vicar, a man highly thought of in his diocese, laid it on with a confidently wielded trowel how unworthy everyone was in the sight of God. At the end of the service, the person next to our friend turned to him, smiling, and asked him if he'd enjoyed the worship. She did not get the answer she was expecting. 'No, I didn't,' he replied, and not only did he explain his feelings to her, he made them clear to the vicar as he left. Good for him, we say.

We also know of a lesbian couple who used to attend the Communion service every Sunday at their parish church. They would come together to the altar rail, kneel and stretch out their hands to receive the bread. Each time the priest would pass them by.

In the name of Christ (irony of ironies!) we still persist in banging the nails into his hands, and apart from the pain we bring upon God, we do so much damage to other people, also.

The socialization and teaching of moral values in our society, both outside and sometimes inside the Church, still depend too often and too heavily on scolding, punishment and chastising of wrong behaviour, and not enough on praising and rewarding of good behaviour. This encourages from a very early age the notion, 'I am flawed and faulty by nature.' On this premise we can develop some very unsatisfactory and unhelpful rules for living that become highly habitual. They become so habituated that they become core beliefs. This happens to the extent that they form a framework for our perception of our world; everything we see is through this murky lens. Our self-speak thinking responses to events, especially ones we don't like, emerge out of this framework.

Sometimes our pattern of self-speak emerges as a reaction to particular events, objects or situations. When these events, objects or situations reoccur, so does the associated self-speak. This process is not as profound as the framework, but is the outworking of it, in response to frequently occurring events. Beck calls them 'negative automatic thoughts' (NATs). Another influential psychologist, Albert Ellis, suggests that human beings naturally have a tendency to think negatively about themselves; how true this is is debatable. Few, however, would argue about the prevalence of guilt, fear and deprecation in people's self-speak.

If we then refer back to the Four Button Model (see Figure 1, p. 12), we can see that any change in one button brings about changes in the others. The occurrence of NATs will result in a lowering of mood and emotions, will have an influence on our biological and physiological state, and will be expressed in our behaviour. In the model the components are simultaneously interdependent and interactive.

Yet we are not victims of our past; however much we are significantly influenced by it, we are not defined by it. As Paul says in 1 Corinthians 13 (and this is our own translation), 'When I was a child, I spoke as a child, I felt as a child, I thought as a child: now that I have grown up, I have left behind the ways of a child.' We are now going to look at how we can begin to 'leave behind the ways of a child'.

We have already seen how useful it is to be able to differentiate between thoughts and feelings. We may be convinced our team will win a vital match and say, 'We feel success is in the air.' But 'success is in the air' is not an emotion, it's a thought. The true emotions around the match are to do with expectations, excitement, and despondency or joy depending on the result. Becoming practised at this differentiation is very useful. When the wind blows, most will say they simply feel the wind on their faces. The experienced sailor will feel the wind as coming from a particular direction. Most of us hear music and take pleasure from it. The musician will recognize the finer points of pitch, rhythm, harmony and structure. For us the task is linking 'I feel . . .' with 'I think . . .' and 'I do . . .'

Explanation

So we can see that feeling low and the thoughts we have about ourselves and our emotions are interlinked. Feeling low makes us vulnerable to more negative self-speak and thinking badly about ourselves, and that in turn interacts with our being prone to unhappy feelings.

Let us think about how this might work. Imagine we were to give you a new, technically advanced (and very annoying) watch that created a buzzing sensation in your wrist every 30 minutes. Suppose we were to instruct you to record how you were feeling at the beginning of your day, and from then on, every time you get the 30-minute sensation, to say to yourself these words, even though you know them to be untrue: 'I'm a useless, worthless and unlovable person and everybody knows it or thinks it.' In addition, every 30 minutes you also had to tense your face, jaw and fist for 30 seconds. Just think what you might write down at the end of the day about how you were feeling! There could well be a marked difference between the two entries in your notebook, and your second entry would hardly read, 'I feel on top of the world'!

That would simply be the result of an artificial thinking exercise combined with physiological tension. In life, however, reality acts upon us in a similarly interrelated way. Sometimes, for example, our physical and biological state predisposes us to feeling negative. Ken recalls the occasion when he had had the flu and, although he was over it, he felt washed out and pathetic. Feeling low is a common consequence of some forms of influenza. We are also more likely to feel a bit low, fragile and tired when we have had relentless stress at work, or when we are managing a seemingly intractable family situation. These physical and emotional states can have an adverse effect on our decision-making and on our biological condition, once again giving a spin to the vicious circle.

At the same time we remain individuals. Some people react with stoic pragmatism to circumstances that would reduce others to a quivering jelly. Like beauty, the nature of a set of circumstances is in the eye of the beholder.

Does it matter if we can identify and quantify each and every influential factor? In our opinion, not a lot. What is critical is the recognition that our emotional, physical, biological and behavioural components interact with each other, and that we are constantly responding to environmental influences. If those influences make us feel pathetic, it doesn't mean we *are* pathetic. And it most certainly does not mean we are deeply, irredeemably and inexplicably flawed. We can make a difference to our lives.

If we can tease out an explanation of what is going on in terms of the process our system is using, we can begin to understand why we feel the way we do. Then our feelings become less of a mystery and we are more able to put in place experiments for coping. The next decision is to try experiments.

Acceptance and adjustment

The twentieth-century American theologian Reinhold Niebuhr composed a short prayer that has justly become famous:

> God, give us grace to accept with serenity the things that cannot be changed,
> courage to change the things that should be changed,
> and the wisdom to distinguish the one from the other.

But to make the decision between acceptance and adjustment is in itself an act of acceptance. Things are different. You have recognized that there is something you would like to be changed, and have thought about giving yourself permission. You are no longer trapped in helplessness.

If you decide that you are willing to accept that this is the situation in which you find yourself, that is a mature thing to do. If you decide that the cost of change to yourself and others is, or might be, too great a price to pay, that is a decision to be respected. Acceptance is not helplessness. Acceptance itself is a change!

If, on the other hand, you would like to make adjustments, so that things might be different, then we move on to Coaching to try experiments.

It is useful to think, at this stage, how you might like life to be as a consequence of the experiments. In this respect, 'better' as opposed to 'unwell' is not an idea we find useful. It's too either/or, on/off. We would prefer goals that are more based on function; for example: 'I would like to be confident enough to volunteer to do something in my local community or with a charity or political party, or in my church.' 'I would like to be able to get better sleep.' 'I would like to be a bit calmer, and less angry, when someone says something I don't like.'

Your goals have to be yours, not ours or anyone else's. Trevor and Ken are mature professional white men; it would be truly impertinent for us to suggest detailed goals to, for example, a young woman from a different cultural background.

These goals can give you something specific to aim for as an objective of your adjustments. It may be helpful to write these goals down and review them from time to time to see if they have been reached or need to change.

Coaching

Going back to the Four Buttons, we recall that the way we behave influences our biological state, which in turn influences how we feel.

In these exercises we are confronting two unhelpful ways of seeing ourselves. The first is the attitude that goes with thoughts such as, 'I can't help it', 'It just happens and there is nothing I can do about it', 'I've always been this way, I can't change' – what one psychiatrist called the helpless-spaniel view of yourself, lying on your back with your legs in the air. This attitude is a choice we can make about our lives, but it has particular consequences. We develop a thought pattern and habit of helplessness that dampens enthusiasm for life and can make us vulnerable to feeling depressed.

The second attitude being confronted is to do with faith, but faith turned toxic: our feeling unhappy must be because of our sin. 'Everyone has sinned, but especially me,' we say, 'and therefore God means me to be unhappy.' On many occasions, in both the Old and New Testaments, there are references to God's ambition for us to have a fulfilled and joyful life. 'I came that they may have life, and have it abundantly,' John's Jesus puts it in John 10.10, and the Parable of the Two Brothers in Luke 15 becomes an invitation to God's party, a party thrown by a God who has shown himself to be absurdly generous and forgiving. What might joining God's party or living life abundantly be like? These exercises might help us find out.

The exercises are *experiments*, and only that. The notion of experiment is critical. What we are discussing is not a prescription, nor a promise: 'Do this and all will be well.' They are experiments. We are inviting you to try something different and see what works for you. We cannot live your life for you, nor can we get inside your own experience of life. We can say there is good research-based evidence that these exercises of trying different ways of thinking and behaving have helped a significant number of people improve the quality of their lives. In the words of a 1950s radio programme, 'Have a Go'.

What follows is a series of interlinked and progressive exercises, which may help us to bring about change. A chart is matched with each exercise, and readers are invited to copy these out and complete them as a way of engaging with the exercise. The exercises in the text below contain a short narrative version corresponding to each of the sheets.

Experiment 1

Keep a diary for a short period, probably between four and six days. Make a regular timed entry, about every three hours, and record your emotional level from 1 to 10 (1 = bad, 10 = good). Then record briefly what you are doing at the time; then what you are thinking. It could begin something like this.

> 9.00 a.m., feeling fed up, score 4; in the car on the way to work and stuck in traffic. Thinking, 'I've got too much to do today. I'll have to work late to get it all done, and I'll miss my evening out. This always happens to me whenever I plan to enjoy myself; something always gets in the way.'

> 12.00 noon, even more fed up, score 3. I'm sitting at my desk, and the computer has just stopped talking to the printer. Thinking I'll never get my work finished now. I'm fated, locked in this circle of underachieving and being unhappy for ever.

> 3.00 p.m., Bill has just taken some files to sort out, as a favour; and the secretary will do the printing. Bill must think I'm OK, he didn't have to offer, and the secretary is willing to help. I might get home in time after all.

Fred did this exercise but instead of prose in a diary he found it easier to do it in chart form (see Table 4.1, overleaf).

There are several skills you develop in doing this:

- You become better at recognizing the difference between thoughts and feelings and differentiating between them.
- You develop the skill of rating the level of a feeling.
- You develop the technique of labelling or naming your feelings.

All this enables your feelings and emotions to be a part of you that you can work with, rather than something that happens to you. More importantly, you can begin to see how your thoughts interact and reciprocate with your feelings; having a thought can result in particular feelings and feelings can predispose you to certain thoughts.

You can imagine people stuck in traffic saying, 'I feel I'm going to be late for work.' But there is no such emotion as 'late for work'. We may feel anxious, frustrated, or even pleased about being late, but 'late for work' is a thought, with an emotion attached that can vary in rating according to how we regard work that day. A glance at the Four Buttons will remind you of the mechanics of this.

You can now do this for yourself. You can use headings in the Thought record 1 chart (Table 4.2, p. 53) or just write it as a prose diary entry.

Which method you use is up to you, as long as it is one you feel comfortable with. The essential part is to be sure that you cover all the column headings of 'Time' through to 'Rate feeling'.

Now see if you can spot a link, theme or relationship between thoughts, feelings, time and situation.

Experiment 2

This is similar to the first, but with some vital differences. We will be looking at how we can manage and influence our own emotions and thoughts. The most important component of this is **evidence**. We described unhelpful self-speak as imperative, absolute and judgemental. In our two imaginary diary

Table 4.1 Thought record 1 – Fred's example

Time	Feeling	Rate feeling from 1 (bad) to 10 (good)	Doing	Thoughts
09.00	Fed up	4	In the car on the way to work and stuck in traffic.	I have got too much to do today. I'll have to work late to get it all done and will miss my evening out. This always happens to me whenever I plan to enjoy myself. Something always gets in the way.
12.00	Even more fed up	3	Sitting at my desk and my computer has just stopped talking to the printer.	I'll never get my work today finished. I am fated, locked in this circle of underachieving and being unhappy for ever.
15.00	Less fed up	7	Bill has just taken some files to sort out for me as a favour and the secretary will do the printing on his computer.	Bill must think I'm OK, he didn't have to offer to sort out those files and the secretary seemed to want to help. I might get home in time after all.

Table 4.2 Thought record 1

Time	Feeling	Rate feeling from 1 (bad) to 10 (good)	Doing	Thoughts

entries the active ingredients of such thinking and the ones that have the most impact are: 'Whenever I plan to enjoy myself something always gets in the way,' or, 'I'm fated, locked in this circle of underachieving and being unhappy for ever.' They are the ones that contain elements of the triad, and which have the potential to begin a vicious circle: negative thoughts lead to feelings of fed-up-ness and depression, which themselves lead to lack of energy, and to behaviour that disposes us to think negatively.

So what is the evidence that supports, 'something always gets in the way of my plans to enjoy myself'? There are two ways of checking the evidence for this, historically and predictively. Have you ever made plans to enjoy yourself and they have been fulfilled? When was the last time you planned an enjoyable activity and it happened? (It is useful to be specific here, because as we have seen in earlier chapters one person's enjoyment can be another's distress.) So when did you last plan to go out for a meal with a friend and it happened and you enjoyed the occasion? When did you last plan to go to a concert or simply go out for a walk and it happened and you enjoyed it? So the absolute contents of the thought 'something always gets in the way of my plans to enjoy myself' can be tested against the evidence and found to be not *absolutely* true. It might be true today, but the reality of today is a one-off. The second check is predictive: how does being stuck in a traffic jam when you have a busy day ahead and might have to change your plans for the evening mean that this will always happen in the future and you will never enjoy yourself again?

Let's see what happens to your mood if you can pay attention to the evidence for the thoughts you have while stuck in a traffic jam. The situation is the same as in Exercise 1; the difference is your consideration, or evaluation, of the evidence for the thoughts you have. Your evaluation will activate change. You look at the evidence for the thoughts that come into your head, and you think, 'Went out last week on Wednesday to the match, had great fun . . . When I think about it, some work could wait till first thing tomorrow. The secretary helped last time we had a work jam; maybe he will today.'

The feelings that result from this thought are less stressful and distressing, more realistic and more hopeful about the future, with perhaps an 8 score.

So try writing such diary entries for a few days, and as you are doing so think about the evidence that supports the absolute, imperative and judgemental components of your thoughts. Write this evidence down at the same time, and then see if focusing on the evidenced thinking influences how you are feeling. Try to keep it ordinary and everyday. The thought, 'Lousy day, didn't do a thing that was of any worth or enjoyment' feels flat and sad. But, the reflection on the evidence for the day is, 'Not done much today, but went to buy a paper and met Bill outside shop. He's been unwell, seemed really pleased to see me, had a few minutes chat'; or, 'Ordered new CD – will enjoy that!' Not such a lousy day after all. For some reason, despite the grace of God, despite the fact that if we read the beginning of Genesis carefully, we will notice it's not about Original Sin, but Original *Blessing*, we seem predisposed to think negatively about ourselves. If we look at the evidence, however, we can positively affect our emotions.

First let's look at Fred's example (see Table 4.3).

Table 4.3 Thought record 2 – Fred's example

Time	Feeling	Rate feeling from 1 (bad) to 10 (good)	Doing	Thoughts	Evidence to support thought	New feeling	Rate new feeling from 1 (bad) to 10 (good)
09.00	Fed up	4	In the car on the way to work and stuck in traffic.	I have got too much to do today. I'll have to work late to get it all done and will miss my evening out. This always happens to me whenever I plan to enjoy myself. Something always gets in the way.	Went out last week on Wednesday to the match, had great fun. Think about priorities of demand and some work could wait till first thing tomorrow. The secretary helped last time we had a work jam, maybe he will today.	Less fed up, more realistic and less hopeless about the future.	8
12.00	Even more fed up	3	Sitting at my desk and my computer has just stopped talking to the printer.	I'll never get my work today finished. I am fated, locked in this circle of underachieving and being unhappy for ever.	Everyone has IT difficulties from time to time, I am not the only one; and it doesn't reflect on my ability to do my job. I'll send an email to see if others are also locked out of their printers.	A bit miffed and frustrated. But relieved it is not necessarily indicative of my performance and a possible solution helps.	7

You can now do this for yourself. At first it might seem a bit stiff and awkward, but once you get into the habit, it becomes an automatic way of viewing your world. You can use the Thought record 2 chart as a model (see Table 4.4), just write it as a prose diary entry or photocopy it to write in. Which method you use is up to you, as long as it is one you feel comfortable with. As with Experiment 1, the essential part is to be sure that you cover all the column headings of 'Time' through to 'Rate new feeling'.

These two exercises, or better called experiments, are essentially about thinking, and the relationship between thinking and feelings. But there is also another strategy that can be used that is behavioural and active in nature and taps into a fundamental part of being human.

Experiment 3

Let's see if we can be a bit more proactive. Research, as well as common sense, suggests that if we do anything we enjoy, we are likely to lift our mood. We can, therefore, regard doing things we see as pleasurable, and which we are reasonably good at, as an antidote to feeling miserable. Being active and being adept even at very small things, which might seem to others inconsequential, is good for our well-being. Installing such activities as part of our daily lives is similar to ensuring that we have a balanced diet. Just as we need food that is not only nutritious in having protein, carbohydrates and fibre but also includes the necessary trace elements, so we need to do things that give us a sense of mastery and pleasure as part of our daily lives.

There are two problems that can arise with doing this activity-oriented looking after ourselves. First, when we are feeling a bit low, we can find it hard to recognize that we are good at anything. Our celebrity-focused culture doesn't help, either. It is easy to think that the only people with talent are those who are famous, or are 'high achievers'. This is a lie. Trevor once visited a woman named Sarah in hospital and took her

Table 4.4 Thought record 2

Time	Feeling	Rate feeling from 1 (bad) to 10 (good)	Doing	Thoughts	Evidence to support thought	New feeling	Rate new feeling from 1 (bad) to 10 (good)

communion. It was a small psycho-geriatric hospital, and Sarah was usually on her own in the ward, or very nearly so. The other patients were generally well enough to be taken to the day-room, where they could at least have some company. Perhaps there would be an old man muttering to himself a few beds up from Sarah, but she had no chance of conversation. She had a son who lived locally, but she never mentioned him coming to see her. She was in a good deal of pain much of the time. But when Trevor asked her what or who she would like to pray for that day, she always had a story to tell about one of the other patients. She seemed utterly devoid of self-pity. When finally Trevor bade her farewell because he was moving to another post, he told her she was an inspiration to him, and always would be. She looked at him with blank incomprehension. That was over 40 years ago, and here we are telling her story! Sarah was good, indeed she was outstanding, at being human.

The second problem is this: it is sometimes regarded as not quite Christian to do things you enjoy and that give you pleasure, even if you know full well that no one else is hurt or harmed in the process. Puritanism is still around, and invariably claims, as it always has, to be based on the Bible. In truth it represents a distortion of biblical teaching. After all, the first miracle Jesus performs in John's Gospel is at a party, and his actions allow the festivities to continue well into the night and beyond. And that story of the wedding at Cana has to be understood against the background of passages in the Old Testament that speak of God laying on a rich feast for his people, 'a feast of rich food, a feast of well-aged wines', as one passage in Isaiah 25.6 puts it.

So for the first part of this exercise, write a list of the little everyday things (about half a dozen) you do that give you some pleasure, and which you think you are quite good at, not the best in the world, just good at (it can be something as ordinary as washing up, or playing with the cat). Now, before you rest for the night, rate your general feeling about the day, between 1 and 10 (with 10 being high), and make a note of it in a diary. Next day, make sure as far as possible that you shut these activities from your mind, and then make another diary note of your feelings. On the third day, make sure you do your activities, and then see if the trace element of the activities influences your feelings. Make a third diary note.

In the second part of the exercise, for the next day that is typical of your normal routine, write down the main activity you do in each hour in just three or four words (for me at this hour, 'at computer writing book'). Do this for each hour of the day you are awake, even if the activity is passive. At the end of the day, or the next day, think about each activity from two perspectives: first, how much did you enjoy it, i.e. what pleasure did you get from it (P); second, how good do you think you were at it, i.e. mastery (M). Then rate each hour from each perspective, between 1 and 10, with 10 being high.

Let's give an example. Ken is phenomenally good at washing up – he was taught as a boy by his grandmother. She had learnt the task while 'in service' in a posh house in the 1880s. His mastery of washing up would be, modestly put, between 8 and 9; his pleasure in washing up somewhat less, at 3–4. On the other hand, his pleasure in sailing a boat is usually very high (7–8) and his mastery between 3 and 4 (safe and competent but hardly competitive in racing or endurance terms).

Now we would like you to rate each entry in terms of M & P (mastery and pleasure). These don't have to be big things, just your everyday activities: washing up, doing the weeding, routine tasks at work, for example. Table 4.5 (overleaf) may help to show what we mean, but as before only use it if it is helpful. We have completed some entries as examples.

Make yourself some blank M & P charts (see Table 4.6, p. 61), or photocopy the table to write in, and try to do this exercise for two or three more days. Then have a look at the pattern and see what activities give you the highest scores. Finally, as

Table 4.5 Example of an M & P chart

Hour	7.00	8.00	9.00	10.00	11.00	12.00	13.00	14.00
Activity	Making and having breakfast							
M & P	M = 3 P = 7							

Hour	15.00	16.00	17.00	18.00	19.00	20.00	21.00	22.00
Activity	Meeting with Jack to discuss solving a problem			Driving home in traffic		Game of squash with Jill		
M & P	M = 7 P = 6			M = 6 P = 2		M = 3 P = 8		

Table 4.6 M & P chart

Hour	7.00	8.00	9.00	10.00	11.00	12.00	13.00	14.00
Activity								
M & P								

Hour	15.00	16.00	17.00	18.00	19.00	20.00	21.00	22.00
Activity								
M & P								

in the first part of the exercise, rate each day overall between 1 and 10, with 10 being high.

Having seen which activities get the higher M & P rating, for three days ensure that at least one of the higher-rated activities gets included each morning, afternoon and evening. Then again rate each day from 1 to 10. Does the inclusion of higher-rated activities make a difference? If it does, try to do a high M & P activity as frequently as you can in your day. In this way you can take some responsibility for how you are feeling; it is not just down to fate, or how people choose to behave towards you.

Following this exercise, from your notes see if there is a connection between doing things you enjoy and things you are good at and how you feel about yourself and the day. To give an example, people who have busy working lives sometimes find it difficult when they retire. At work they did things they were good at, and met people who contributed to their social life. How they replace all this when they no longer go to work influences how they feel.

Experiment 4

This experiment is both biological and behavioural. To do it, you will need at least one day when you don't need to work, and, if you have a spouse or partner, they will need to be understanding and supportive. Its objective is to test what happens to your feelings if you deliberately behave differently on two separate days. Again, you will need to rate them.

The exercise requires two successive days. On day one, assuming you are in reasonable physical health, get up, wash, get dressed and have a good breakfast. Make sure you do some physical exercise you enjoy, even if it is only a brief walk. Eat a balanced diet with fresh, home-prepared food. If you drink caffeine drinks, do not have more than three or four cups of tea, coffee or cola drinks. If you would normally have an alcoholic drink, make sure it is within the recommended limits (a visit to <www.drinkaware.co.uk> will give you more information if you need it). If you usually spend time in prayer or contemplation, make sure you put this into your day. In other words, without making any undue effort, have a purposeful and active day. If you are not as healthy as you would like to be, you can still try to have such a day within the constraints of your health. At the end of the day, rate how you feel.

The second day is quite different. Do the opposite of the previous day: slouch about the place, don't take care of yourself, and do very little, especially nothing physical. Again rate the day, and note the difference between the ratings.

If you rated the day you took care of yourself – when you did some exercise together with prayer and/or contemplation – higher than the day you slouched about, then that tells you something about yourself. If it was the other way round, that also may be saying something to you about your life.

Evaluation

This is an important part of the experiment. Remember that earlier we looked at the idea that the only experiments that fail are the ones that do not tell us anything, not the ones that do not work out as we hoped. If the experiments above have told you something about how you can cope with negative thinking, then it has been a successful exercise. Think back to your goals. If you have moved towards these by virtue of using an experiment, you have learnt something about the consequences of using a particular coping strategy. If you have not moved towards them, then you can review how the experiment can be done differently or find an alternative. You have learnt a bit about what works for you and how you can try to inoculate yourself against the consequences arising from your perception of distressing events in future. If nothing has changed, you have, at the very least, given yourself permission to try to make a difference, and so can go on developing your own experiments.

5

'Consider the lilies of the field':
anxiety

'Don't do theology, dear'

'Don't do theology, dear, it'll ruin your faith.' A mother to her son when he was about to go away to university. She was afraid for her son, afraid of him leaving home for the first time, afraid of cutting the strings and letting him fly, afraid of what might become of him at university and what might happen to him, afraid of allowing him to grow up and become a fully fledged adult. All those fears and anxieties were present in her words, though they weren't expressed, or even acknowledged by her. She was generally a rather anxious person, but she couldn't admit that to herself either. For anxiety was a sin in her eyes. Had not Jesus said in the Sermon on the Mount that we were not to be anxious? *Five times* he said it. 'You of little faith,' he called the people listening to him. So anxiety was a sign of a lack of faith in God, a not trusting in God and his fatherly goodness.

As far as that mother was concerned, the text of Matthew's Gospel was quite plain: anxiety was a sin, so better to pretend that all was well, or else offer up an arrow prayer to God and sort it that way. Don't admit to being anxious, because then you have to face up to your sinfulness, and that is hard to do, because sin cuts you off from God, and you don't want to be cut off from God. Don't admit to being afraid, either, for doesn't the Bible also say, 'perfect love casts out fear'? Yes, it does, in 1 John 4.18, in that famous passage about the love of God and our loving him back in return. 'We love because he first loved us,' it says just one verse later. Exactly. So if we're afraid, we can't be loving God, or not loving God enough, at least. And if we're not loving God, then that's *seriously* sinful.

'Don't do theology, dear, it'll ruin your faith.' Those were the words she dared to speak, and though beneath them lay so many layers of fear, they voiced another, more immediate anxiety. To that mother, having faith in God meant trusting God completely, and that meant never having doubts, never questioning. Doubt, too, was a sin, and questions would inevitably lead to it. She didn't know what went on in university theological departments, but she'd heard about those fancy new theologians and their dangerous nonsense. She didn't want her son to be led astray by them.

The son did what he was told. He went away to study something else instead. For two years. His university, however, made it easy for students to change subjects part-way through the course. Up at college, away from his mother, he began to find and enjoy his independence. And he met some teachers of theology and found them invigorating. After two years he changed to theology. He jumped in with both feet, and found he was in his element. His faith was never the same again. In his eyes it was more vibrant and exciting, much deeper than before. But he knew his mother would never understand. She would just think her worst fears had come true. So, without saying anything to each other, they agreed not to discuss it. It was sad, since her faith was so important to her, and his faith was so important to him.

Eventually, in her eighties, she got Parkinson's disease, and lost the power to communicate. Except through her eyes. And her eyes told a remarkable tale. One might almost call it a miracle: the Parkinson's allowed her to break through the narrow confines of her faith, escape those elements of it, at least, that had held her in thrall for so long. She was free! She had, we might say, found the unconditional love of God, at last. Perfect love *had* cast out fear. But it was too late to discuss theology with her son.

Perfectly reasonable anxiety

Let's think a bit more about what's happening in this story. First, there's a perfectly ordinary and reasonable anxiety: a son was about to flee the nest into the big wide world. What's worse, it was a world of which his parents had no experience. Neither of them had been to university, nor had any other member of the wider family. Most parents in these circumstances would have apprehensions and anxiety. After all, the mother had looked after her son for over 18 years, knowing and anticipating, usually successfully, what would come next in both his daily routine and his life. She had got into the habit of caring for him; she couldn't just turn off the caring at the beginning of a university term. She didn't know what would befall him, and because he was so far away, she was no longer in a position to put things right if they did go wrong. Perhaps those who say, 'Don't worry, just trust the Lord,' do not know what it's like being a parent. For most parents, being concerned about their children is life-long, normal, entirely natural. It's a terminal condition.

There was another component, however, to the anxiety of this particular mother. Her faith was so vital to her very being, that just as she would want her son to eat, sleep and keep warm, so she would also want him to keep the faith they shared. Faith was not to be questioned, and losing it had dire consequences, or so she believed. No wonder she had forebodings for his future. If he studied theology, she thought, he would be exposed to clever people who doubted and questioned everything, academics who saw every truth as relative and destroyed certainty. If this happened, he could end up rudderless in life; or, even worse, there could develop a fissure between them, and she could lose her relationship with her son.

Represented in this story are two aspects of anxiety. One is what we might call usual biological instinct, which is perfectly natural – in this case the normal response to children separating from their parents. The other is based on thinking, speculation and 'what if-ing', something we might call 'worst-case-scenario' anxiety. Most anxiety seems to contain elements of these two positions.

'Therefore I tell you, do not be anxious'

But surely we can't escape the Sermon on the Mount, can we? That passage on anxiety in Matthew 6.25–34 (with its parallel in Luke 12.22–32) repeats the phrase 'do not be anxious' three times, in verses 25, 31 and 34 (see the RSV translation). 'Look at the birds of the air,' Jesus says. 'They neither sow nor reap nor gather into barns, and yet your heavenly father feeds them' (6.26). He also seems to claim that anxiety is useless: 'And can any of you by being anxious add a single hour to your span of life?' (6.27). In the next verse he asks, 'And why are you anxious about clothing?' and he continues with those justly famous words:

> Consider the lilies of the field, how they grow; they neither toil nor spin, yet I tell you, even Solomon in all his glory was not clothed like one of these. But if God so clothes the grass of the field, which is alive today and tomorrow is thrown into the oven, will he not much more clothe you – you of little faith?
>
> (Matthew 6.28–30)

No, we can't escape those verses, but we can seek to get inside the world of which they speak.

Their style is somewhat combative. We might think Jesus is being rather hard on his hearers. We might prefer something a bit more gentle, or polite, less likely to make anyone blush with shame. But we must remember that Jesus was a Jew, and regarded by some of his Jewish contemporaries as a prophet, as both Matthew and Luke testify (see Matthew 14.5 and Luke 7.16). The prophets whose poetry has come down to us in the Old Testament are not exactly noted for their gentleness of tone, or for pussyfooting around their audiences or the subjects they address. They tell it straight and they tell it strong. Think of Amos, of Isaiah or Jeremiah, for just three. All four Gospels present us with a Jesus who belongs to the ancient Jewish prophetic tradition. Of course, they find him much more than a prophet, but like the prophets before him he told it straight and he told it strong. In putting these sayings about anxiety back into the world from which they came, we have to recognize first the rhetorical landscape: the splendid Jewish culture of no-nonsense speaking to which they belong.

We then have to acknowledge the social and economic world they first inhabited. Jesus is talking here about the very basics of human life: food, drink and clothing. (He might have added shelter to the list, but often storytellers work in threes; Jesus was a marvellous storyteller, and so was Matthew.) Yet we could argue that this only makes things worse. Was Jesus a rich person, then, who had never needed for anything, and could not understand what life was like for the majority of his disciples? We know full well this is not true. Jesus was brought up in a small Jewish peasant village, where no rich people lived. As one commentator has put it, peasant life in first-century Galilee rested uneasily 'on a narrow margin between subsistence and abject poverty'.[12] Growing up in Nazareth, Jesus would have known many days when his family and his neighbours did not know where the next meal was coming from. If those who study mortality rates in the ancient world are right, then perhaps almost a third of the children he played with as a boy did not reach the age of six, and another third died before they were 16. They died as a result of hunger or disease. So Jesus can have had no illusions about poverty, or about the fears and anxieties it brought with it. He will have known, also, the sheer unremitting toil involved for parents trying to feed and clothe their families. No doubt, as he grew up, he would have shared in that work himself, as children still do in many countries.

So when he says to his disciples, 'Therefore do not be anxious, saying, "What shall we eat?" or "What shall we drink?" or "What shall we wear?"' (Matthew 6.31, RSV), has he taken leave of his senses, slipped over into madness? No, not that either. Both Matthew and Luke represent Jesus as addressing these words to his followers, to those who were literally following him from place to place. The Church has generally portrayed Jesus as being followed by just 12 men, but when it has done that, it has not been reading its Gospels very carefully. For they tell us his followers were many more than that, and included women, and perhaps children. These had abandoned their farms, villages and towns. The men had left behind their sowing, their reaping and gathering into barns, and the women their spinning and weaving. All of them were taking an enormous risk, but they were not journeying into a void. Following the footsteps of this peasant from Nazareth, they were walking together into the heart of the kingdom of God. Some had left their families behind, but they had joined a new one, the family of God himself. They were God's children, sitting round God's table, wrapped in the warmth of God's cloak of acceptance, forgiveness and unbreakable love.

It was all a matter of priorities. The passage in Matthew builds to this climax: 'Strive first for the kingdom of God and his righteousness, and all these things will be added to you as well' (6.33).

One of us once taught in a public boarding school where the teachers were paid fairly handsomely and many lived in luxurious houses provided for them. When he moved on to teach in a theological college, he halved his previous salary and worked among students, most of them married, surviving on the meagre grants the Church of England could afford. The school had been a fine place in many ways, and its teachers dedicated and extremely hard-working, but many of them and their wives talked constantly about money and their perceived lack of it. In the theological college hardly anyone talked about money, whether they were staff or students, though the students certainly had very little; and since they were hoping to be ordained as priests, they had the prospect of moderate stipends for the rest of their lives. It was, you see, a question of preoccupations and priorities. For those students, seeking first the kingdom of God and his righteousness (a very strange priority in the modern world, as it was in the world of Jesus) put things in a different perspective. A few verses earlier in the Sermon on the Mount, we find:

> Do not store up for yourselves treasures on earth, where moth and rust consume and where thieves break in and steal; but store up for yourselves treasures in heaven, where neither moth nor rust consumes and where thieves do not break in and steal. For where your treasure is, there your heart will be also.
>
> (Matthew 6.19–21)

Exactly.

Anxiety is not *a sin – it can be helpful*

As far as that 'Don't do theology, dear' mother was concerned, the text of Matthew's Gospel was quite plain: anxiety was a sin. We can see now that she was taking the text the wrong way. She had been taught to pick the truth off the surface of the Bible, without delving beneath the words. It was a serious mistake, and a very sad one for her, for it meant she regarded as sinful what is perfectly natural for a caring mum. Being anxious about their children is, after all, what most mums do! If only someone had encouraged her to try giving herself permission to be anxious!

In truth, the problems to do with the notion that 'anxiety is a sin' go far beyond careful interpretation of the Sermon on the Mount. We have already seen that much anxiety is perfectly reasonable. But there is a lot more to be said than that. As a result of our evolution we human beings have a very highly developed and sophisticated dependence on anxiety. All of us alive today have in our background and our genes ancestors who were very effective at coping with dangers of one kind or another. Anxiety was part of a mechanism that helped them survive.

Over 11,000 years ago, Trevor's and Ken's forefathers and foremothers were out for a walk in the forest. They were deep in conversation, and typically, but unwisely, oblivious to their surroundings (a trait still present in their descendants). Suddenly, just ahead, and far too close for comfort, they saw a flash of white emanating from the smile of a sabre-toothed tiger. This was a mortally dangerous position to be in. Trevor's ancestors reached for their weapons, tensed the muscles they would use, fixed a stare, and prepared to do battle. Their heart rate went up, blood coursed through their bodies, they took deep breaths and anticipated the fight. Ken's ancestors saw things very differently: fighting such a large and fierce animal was not a sensible solution; getting out the way was preferable. They decided to make a run for it. They tensed the muscles they would use, fixed a stare, and prepared to run. Their heart rate went up, blood coursed through their bodies, they took deep breaths and anticipated the flight. Because Ken and Trevor are writing this together it is obvious both pairs of ancestors survived.

This deeply embedded response is common to many animals. A friend of ours recently acquired a kitten. She, the kitten, did not need to be shown what to do when she was introduced to a neighbour's dog. Her back arched, her claws were at the ready and there was a great deal of hissing. This response in all animals, including us humans, is known as 'flight and fight'.

And just because we human beings have become clever and sophisticated, it doesn't mean it's no longer an influence on our behaviour. It is still deeply embedded. Last week Trevor and Ken were out for a walk in the town. They were typically deep in conversation and somewhat oblivious to their surroundings.

Ken unwittingly stepped off the kerb. Trevor instinctively, and seemingly instantly, tensed his muscles, fixed a stare, took a deep breath and then, with his heart rate increased and with blood coursing through his body, he grabbed Ken's jacket and pulled him out of the path of a double-decker bus.

Anxiety is fine as a response when the threat is real, be it a sabre-toothed tiger or a double-decker bus that's too close for comfort. Anxiety in this situation triggers essential physical qualities that can help us to survive. It could be described as helpful anxiety, God-given anxiety, meant to enable the species he created to survive and flourish.

Sometimes, of course, it doesn't work, but that is another matter. Sometimes the sabre-toothed tiger wins the fight or catches up with us. We Christians tell an astonishing story of a garden called Gethsemane, when the Son of God threw himself on the ground, 'distressed and agitated', and, 'deeply grieved, even to death', prayed to his Father to save him (Mark 14.32–42). The crowd still found him with their swords and clubs at the ready and a kiss from one of his closest friends, and too soon he found himself nailed to a disgusting cross. But that was not because of his anxiety! It would be grotesque to suggest that Jesus died because his faith in God had collapsed in Gethsemane, or because his anxiety had been sinful. In truth the Gethsemane story, written by Mark with such exquisite restraint, is one of the clearest testimonies in his Gospel to the depth of Jesus' faith and his closeness to his Father.

But . . . problems with our physiology

But what of the other sort, the negative anxiety? This is far more complex, and usually involves cognition, perception and thinking. Unlike the God-given survival anxiety, it tends to be learnt rather than instinctive. We don't have to be told that a house on fire is a danger to our lives, yet some of us behave in a very similar anxious way when facing an examination or a job interview. At one level we know the difference in the consequences: fires can kill; examinations and interviews do not. But we can still use similar language about both. 'My whole life depends on getting two Bs in the final exam!' we say, or 'Getting this job is my last chance in life.'

Because the phenomenon of anxiety is so critical to our survival, and so ingrained in our being, we can use it ubiquitously to motivate ourselves. If we approach the exam, the presentation, or the driving test too laid back and relaxed, and our performance is not up to much, we have not put in enough effort. On the other hand, if we become too stressed and anxious, this can get in the way and the execution of our task will be flawed. In the early part of the twentieth century two scientists called Yerkes and Dodson proposed a law that suggested that there was an optimum level of anxiety, or arousal, to facilitate our achievements. It is called the 'Inverted U Model', and illustrated in Figure 3.

We may have seen, or been, the person who, on a first date, instead of being that suave, amusing, attractive companion, is so overwhelmed with nerves they become a gibbering, incoherent

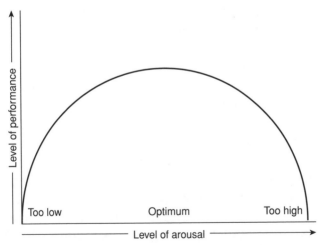

Figure 3 **The Yerkes and Dodson Inverted U Model**

wreck. Yet we also know that to do something special, really well, we have to 'psych ourselves up'; if we don't, we risk being so laid back, it all goes awry.

Much of our anxiety is not centred on actual physical threats, but stems from our thinking and an assessment of threats, which may, or may not, have elements of reality. Typically the language we use of such threats will have ideas of 'what if?' 'must', 'should', 'ought to', 'got to', 'I must be ... or I will be seen to be useless', attached to them. Characteristically the language of these internal thoughts is absolute, imperative and judgemental. Thoughts containing these ideas are appropriate and helpful in avoiding or fighting sabre-toothed tigers, where there is a high, actual and realistic risk of harm, because they provoke the body to respond. For threats that are much less clear-cut, such internal language is often unhelpful because vigorous 'flighting and fighting' are not available. In our sophisticated world more primal methods of dealing with threats are generally unavailable and untenable. For example, hitting the chairperson of the interview panel over the head with a club when we are threatened with a difficult question is unlikely to aid the prospect of getting a job; running out of the room when you don't think you know the answer to an exam question probably guarantees failure.

This is where anxiety can become problematic. The coping strategies we have been given by our Creator through evolution have been fine for most of our evolutionary history. In our complex and modern world, however, what we naturally want to use, 'flight or fight', is usually not available because of social constraints.

We have in our system mechanisms that tell us when to breathe; when our hearts should make the next beat; when our skin should produce sweat; when we need to eat or drink. We humans share these mechanisms with most animals with nerve systems, and evolution has meant that all of us have similarities in our brain and neurological structures that perform these functions. Our friend's newly acquired kitten, as well as reacting to the sight of the dog, can also demand food when her brain tells her she is hungry; similarly her system tells her heart to beat faster when she is chasing a toy mouse and go slower when curled up asleep. Because this is common to so many species it is thought to have developed early on in our evolutionary history, and is sometimes referred to as 'the primitive brain'. The part of our brains where anxiety responses take place is called the hippocampus, and it belongs to this primitive brain. But we humans have much more active brains, with parts that have developed significantly later and with considerably more complexity. These parts are called the cerebral cortex. It is this cerebral cortex that does the thinking, gives meaning, holds much of our memory and makes language happen. At an anatomical and neurological level it is one of the features that make us human. One of the problems we have is to do with the communications systems between the early evolutionary part of our brain and the cerebral cortex. It tends to be one-way: our cerebral cortex can talk to our hippocampus, but there is a very limited service the other way round.

So when we have thoughts that are characterized by 'what if', 'must', 'should', 'ought to', 'got to', 'I must be . . . or I will be seen to be useless', our hippocampus receives the message and starts to activate the anxiety responses engraved on us by evolution; it tells another gland to pump hormones such as adrenalin and neurotransmitters into our systems. If we don't burn these off by either flight or fight behaviour, our hippocampus sends the message, 'give us some more'. As a result we can feel worse, and language like 'I can't stand it' begins to come into play.

The mechanics of anxiety

It's all cyclical. We need to look back at the Four Buttons diagram, to see how the buttons link up when we are feeling anxious or worried. This applies to both short-term and long-term anxiety, to realizing we might be about to step into the path of a double-decker, or to fears about a child of ours about to go to university. The mechanism works largely the same in both situations.

Let us begin with the brain picking up information that there is a threat. This may be an external one, such as a double-decker bus coming towards us, or an internal thought, 'What if my child does theology?' (cognition). The neuro system picks up the information that there is a threat, and secretes adrenalin, together with other hormones, which alter the body's state: our blood pressure rises, our sweat glands function, we get clammy, our breathing becomes faster and more shallow, the hair on our hands, arms and back of the neck stands up, our stomach churns and we want to defecate (physical/biological).

Interestingly enough, part of this process is described at one point in Luke's version of the story of Jesus praying in Gethsemane just before his arrest. The verse concerned (Luke 22.44) doesn't appear in many of the best ancient manuscripts, and may very well not belong to what Luke originally wrote (some translations, such as the NRSV, put it in square brackets). But all that matters here is what it says: 'In his anguish he prayed more earnestly, and his sweat became like great drops of blood falling down on the ground.' From this some people have concluded that Jesus was sweating blood, but the verse is simply describing profuse sweating as a result of extreme anxiety. One highly regarded commentator on Luke, Joseph Fitzmyer, actually translates the beginning of the verse, 'In his *anxiety* he prayed still more earnestly' (our italics).

Such physical or biological symptoms can result in our behaviour changing. We might become less relaxed in our movements, more restless and agitated, even aggressive, or else we may avoid situations, go quiet, hide, and try to pretend that nothing has happened (behaviour). And we have the emotions of fear, anxiety and worry (feelings). The whole cycle can happen in a fraction of a second, just as you put the brakes on before you even think about it, if someone steps into the path of your car.

Because we feel like this, we are more inclined to interpret normal events as threats (cognition). Neutral behaviour in others can be seen as threatening. To cope with the general discomfort, we have a cup of coffee (behaviour). Coffee contains caffeine, which is a stimulant that increases secretion of adrenalin (physical/biological). It's a bit like a pinball game; each button bounces the ball to make other buttons react.

Safety behaviours

Such a range of responses can be called 'safety behaviours'. These are behavioural responses to a threat, or to a perceived threat, that seem to us, instinctively, to be right, but in actuality make matters worse. Safety behaviours almost always involve either tension or avoidance.

Let's consider some examples: tension first. When we slip and think we may fall over, we get tense and try to stop ourselves falling, or we put our hand out to minimize the injuries we could encounter. The slapstick comic actor, the jockey over the jumps, the high-speed skier have all learnt to roll so that when they fall they do not end up with fractured limbs. They have learnt counter-intuitive behaviour. The youth worker, faced with an angry and aggressive teenager in a community centre, may well feel angry herself and disappointed at the young person's immature behaviour. Her instinct is to shout back, but her skill and experience say, 'Keep a level head, don't adopt a belligerent posture, make sure your voice stays calm. That way you will prevent a vicious circle and an escalation of the situation.' The wise mother, although she may at times be tired, frustrated, fed up and want to scream when her toddler acts up in the supermarket, has learnt that scolding and remonstrating with a stroppy two year old just makes matters worse. Both the youth worker and the mother feel anxious at being involved in a public confrontation, and the Four Buttons start their cycle. Their safety behaviours may tell them to hit out, or aggressively assert their authority, but their wisdom tells them this is counterproductive.

The second common type of safety behaviour is avoidance. Remember, safety behaviours make matters worse, although in the heat of the moment we may think they will make them better, or we say we can't help it. University lecturers who teach mature students will frequently have people on their courses who have the ability to do well but are hampered by a bad experience in the classroom at school. Wanting the best for their students, the lecturers offer extra tuition. To their dismay the students who take advantage of the offer are those who don't really need it, while the anxious ones avoid it. We will all have heard of people who feel unwell and think they have a serious illness, and yet do not go to their doctor because they want to avoid bad news. The mother in our opening story was also advocating avoidance, of course: 'Don't do theology, dear, it'll ruin your faith.' In other words, 'Avoid theology, since I see it as a threat to what I hold dear, and it may lead to the catastrophe of a loss of faith.'

Disabling anxiety

Anxiety and fears are rational, normal and natural emotions. As we have seen, in some circumstances they are desirable. Yet they also have the capacity to be very distressing and disabling. Some people seem to be in a constant state of quite high anxiety, which can be annoying for them, but they accommodate it and learn to live with it. Others persistently see threats in quite ordinary events and situations of everyday life, and their anxiety blights their aspirations and confines the abundant life Jesus offers. Some are overwhelmed by sudden attacks of anxiety and become dysfunctional. The emotion gets in the way of their living life as they would wish. Yet others are plagued by a fearful anticipation of the emotion, and become afraid of being afraid.

Unhelpful or disabling anxiety seems to describe a vicious circle, bouncing round the Four Buttons.

What we have here is an **explanation** of how anxiety works, in both its helpful and unhelpful forms.

So what can be done?

Doing something about anxiety means two things: looking at our thinking and our behaviour, and experimenting with changing both.

A psychologist, David Barlow, suggested there are fundamental aspects that are core natural characteristics of anxiety, especially unhelpful anxiety.

1 Typically when we feel anxious, we overestimate the threat. What we see as a threat is too big or too hard for us to deal with, and wishes us harm.
2 Typically when we feel anxious, we overestimate the catastrophe. We may believe we will die or be badly injured, or else will be shamed and looked down on.
3 Typically we underestimate our ability to cope and the resources we can call upon.

If Barlow is right, then this leads to further questions to ask of our thinking.

Estimating the threat

First, is our estimation of the threat proportional and appropriate? What is the evidence to support our estimate? What is the evidence that there really is a threat? If the house is on fire, this is genuinely dangerous, and being afraid of fire is proportional and appropriate. But if we return to the story at the beginning of this chapter, we might wish to ask the anxious mother for the evidence that her son would lose his faith if he did theology. Some people do question their faith on theology courses, but that is not the same as losing it; it just becomes different. Many, in fact, find their faith much enhanced and enriched by their studies. It is true, a few discover that their faith takes a battering from which it does not recover, but where is the evidence that such a threat applied to that woman's son? Was his faith particularly rigid, brittle or fragile before he set off for university? Presumably not, if his studies enriched it in the way the story reports. Note the language of the mother's thinking: 'Don't do theology, dear, it'll ruin your faith.' It's imperative, absolute; it's loaded with 'what ifs'; it's black and white, allowing no gradation. It has the echo of, 'Don't step off the kerb, you'll get knocked down.' No wonder she was anxious! If you recall, as we said in Chapter 1, we are not distressed by things or events but by the way we perceive them. She saw doing theology as dangerous, and therefore something to be anxious about.

Many Christians share her anxieties about academic theology, so many indeed that it is worth dwelling for a moment on the subject before we move on. Too often academic theology is confined to university departments, and does not penetrate the thick stone walls of our churches. As a result, lay people are too often left in the dark, ignorant of what the theologians are really saying, and perhaps even encouraged to be suspicious of them. They are then vulnerable to the sensationalist tabloid press and their occasional rants about some radical scholar or bishop and all their works. Remember the mother of our story had heard about 'those fancy new theologians and their dangerous nonsense'. It's unlikely, alas, that she would have been offered an informed and balanced introduction to their thinking in her home church. 'Don't do theology, dear, it'll ruin your faith' is an attitude she might well have picked up or had reinforced on more than one Sunday.

In some churches Christians are firmly told what to believe, what to think, even what to feel. In many more churches people are not really encouraged to question, or to think for themselves. When the Gospels are preached, they are presented as if they were exact records of events, even when there are clear discrepancies between them. The fact that each of the four evangelists was a creative genius is not so much as hinted at, let alone celebrated to the skies. And the Bible is always *right*. More significantly, it is a very rare church indeed where people are positively encouraged to question *God*, to protest, or to complain to him, when needs must. We are to give thanks to God 'at all times and in all places', as the Book of Common Prayer has it.

And all that is mighty strange, given the nature of the Church's Scriptures. There is a very great deal of prayer in the Bible, speech addressed directly to God. The vast bulk of it is in the Hebrew Scriptures, in what we Christians call the Old Testament. There the prayer of vigorous, sometimes angry protest is very common, as we have already made plain. It lies at the heart of the Old Testament's discourse with God. In the last chapter we gave the example of Psalm 88, a prayer that is prayed in the pitch dark, and whose final word is 'darkness'. Here let us quote the bitter words of Moses that are hurled with such force into the face of God in Exodus 5.22–23: 'My Lord, why have you brought disaster upon this people? Why the hell did you send me? Ever since I came to Pharaoh to speak in your name, he has brought disaster upon this people! And as for rescuing, you have not rescued your people!' (our own translation). When did you last hear a prayer like that prayed in church? We have been taught to be much more polite with God than that, and curiously, much more cautious. Yet not once is such prayer condemned in the Old Testament, at least not by God. When Job brings such fearful accusations against the God he believes has tried to crush him, his companions are deeply unnerved by his language and by the venom with which it is spoken, and sit in high judgement upon him. But when finally God appears on the scene he condemns not Job but the companions for 'not speaking what is right'. He upholds, indeed commends Job for his integrity, his plain speaking, his refusal to pretend or toe the line, his *fearlessness*.

Behind the mother's anxiety about theology, behind her anxiety about *anxiety*, was a deeper anxiety about God. That was not surprising, either. The Church has spent enough time over the centuries putting the fear of God into people, and sometimes it is still engaged in that sorry exercise. The truth is, we really do not need to be afraid of God! God is *love*. God can never be a threat.

Estimating the catastrophe

The second question is this: even if the threat happens, are our estimations of the catastrophe proportional and appropriate? What is the evidence to support our thought? What is the evidence that this threat happening will result in what we are thinking? There is clear evidence that, unless they are appropriately attired, firefighters entering a burning house are very likely to suffer serious injury or death. Mobilizing their anxiety mechanisms of flight and fight is appropriate and proportional. On the other hand, the mother's deep-seated anxiety about the catastrophe of her son, or herself, being cut off from God was neither proportional nor appropriate.

In Chapter 3, and again briefly in the last chapter, we spoke of the Parable of the Two Brothers in Luke 15. The story swirls with anxiety. Imagine the fears of the younger son as he sets out to return to his village. He has brought shame on his father, his family, his whole village. He can expect people to gather when they see him coming, and they won't be glad to see him back. He can expect the wrath of his family and especially his father, whom he so humiliated when he asked for his share of his inheritance. That request, put so bluntly in Luke's text, was tantamount to wishing his father dead. He knows how much he insulted him then, and now he comes back with nothing. Everything he took with him to that foreign country he has lost. He presumes he will never be accepted back into the family. The best he can hope for is that his father will take him on as a hired hand. That way he will be able to keep his distance from his hostility – because surely his father must hate him – but if he is hired, at least he will have something to eat. He works out in advance what to say when he meets him: 'Father, I have sinned against heaven and before you; I am no longer worthy to be called your son; treat me like one of your hired hands' (Luke 15.18–19). Then, however, as we all know, his father runs up the road to meet him, and before he can utter a word of his speech he throws his arms around him and kisses him! We Christians, indeed people of other faiths also, have always had difficulty in coming to terms with the forgiveness of God. It is given so freely, in such full measure, even when we don't deserve an ounce of it! It always far exceeds expectations.

The anxiety of the older son in the second half of the parable is half hidden behind his fury. When he comes on the scene the party for his brother is already in full swing. He doesn't know what is going on and has to ask a young slave. He is an outsider at this point in the story, both literally and metaphorically. He stands outside the house where the feast is taking place, and he feels detached from his father, who has gone ahead without him, and from the family and the larger community who are all inside enjoying themselves. He can hear the sound of music and dancing, but he is not a part of it. When he learns from the slave that his father has thrown a lavish feast in honour of his brother, he feels even more excluded. The extent of his feelings is made plain when he confronts his father. 'Listen!' he cries. 'For all these years I have been working like a slave for you, and I have never disobeyed your command; yet you have never given me even a young goat so that I might celebrate with my friends. But when this son of yours came back' (notice he doesn't call him 'my brother'), 'who has devoured your property with prostitutes' (how does he know that? He doesn't; it is his hurt and anger talking) 'you killed the fatted calf for him!' (Luke 15.29–30).

He too, in fact, humiliated his father near the beginning of the story, when his father gave him his share of the family estate. He should have refused it, for acceptance would seem to imply that he also wished his father dead. And he should have used his authority as the elder son to try and persuade his brother to abandon his plans. Does the memory of that now haunt him when his father emerges from the feast to plead with him? He is certainly extremely anxious about his status in the family and his relationship with his father in particular. Has his father really been treating him like a slave all these years? Surely the picture the parable presents of the father would rule that out. And yet he *feels* he has. He feels utterly rejected, and he projects those feelings back into the past. 'It has always been like this!' he says to himself. 'And it will always be like this! I will always be an outsider, left out of the party, separated from my brother, at odds with my father, and never enjoying the privileges of an elder son.' And to this, as again we know already, his father says, 'Child, you are always with me, and all that is mine is yours.' He *is* the elder son, after all! Though his brother has been dressed up for the feast in his father's best robe and is wearing his father's signet ring on his finger, though he is, in other words, looking for all the world like an elder son, indeed one already in charge of things, he, the elder son, still hears his father say, 'all that is mine is *yours*'. It makes no sense at all.

At the end the Parable of the Two Brothers leaves us with *two* elder brothers: at least, to be precise, with two men enjoying at the same time the privileges and status of a first-born son. It is deliberate, playful and most glorious nonsense, for it shows us that any anxiety we might have about living up to God's impossible standards, or about his excluding, rejecting or condemning us, is misplaced. God can never regard us as anything other than his precious children. And indeed, if he really does dress us up in his best robe, or say to us, 'all that is

84

mine is yours', he treats us as his treasured companions, his friends, his colleagues. He treats us as if (dare we say this?) we were his equals! What extraordinary nonsense is *that*?

With God there can be no catastrophe.

Acceptance

So we have reached the matter of **acceptance**: acceptance that the distress I am experiencing emotionally and physically, the distress that affects the quality of my life, is not there because I am a deeply flawed, inadequate person, or because there is something wrong with me, or because I have sinned against the will and purpose of God. It is a natural and normal response to events in my life. The fact that it is natural does not make it desirable, or inevitable, or the cross I have to bear. We can do something about it. That is another thing we can come to accept. We can do something about it! We can **adjust**.

Adjusting: a story and an experiment

This is a story about Dave and Jean, who for years had been close friends. Then there's Margaret and Bill. Dave and Bill had known one another since school days, and all four of them belonged to the same rambling club and went to the same church.

Dave and Jean began to notice a change in Margaret and Bill. On the club walks they somehow always managed to be together. At the pub lunches they would invariably sit beside one another, and the same in church on Sunday. They seemed unusually relaxed and happy in each other's company. There was a new glint in their eyes. Dave and Jean didn't say anything, but it came as no surprise when Margaret and Bill announced they were getting married. However, it came as a shock to Dave when Bill asked him to be his best man. He felt flattered, honoured, delighted to be asked . . . and terrified. He'd have to make a speech at the reception! He could never do such a thing.

He'd been to the weddings of many friends over the years, but never been a best man before. He was not married himself, so he hadn't had to give the groom's speech, either. When Bill asked him, his mind fled straight back to his school days, to a particular day and a particular lesson. He'd never forgotten it.

They were studying the First World War in history and in English, and the English teacher had set one of the poems of Wilfred Owen, the war poet, for them to write about as their homework. When the next English lesson came, the teacher started a discussion of the poem. 'Higgins,' she said (this was Dave's second name), 'stand up and recite "Strange Meeting". No, don't look at the book. Do it from memory. You said in your homework what an impression it had made on you. Now let's see how deep that impression was.'

Dave had long thought this teacher didn't like him much. She hadn't told them they had to *learn* the poem. She was picking on him. It was unfair. And the poem was quite long. He stood up. Looking down at his desk, staring at the closed book of poems, he began, 'It seemed that out of battle I escaped . . .'

'Speak up!' the teacher said. 'We can't hear you.'

'It seemed that out of battle I escaped / Down some profound tunnel . . .'

'Profound *dull* tunnel!' the teacher cried. 'Miss out the "dull" and you change the sense to nonsense and lose all rhythm. Have you no feeling for poetry, Higgins? Again!'

'It seemed that out of battle I escaped / Down some profound dull tunnel, dug / Through granites . . .'

'Dug through granites?' The teacher was shouting now. '"*Long since scooped* / Through granites"! There's all the difference in the world between "dug" and "long since scooped"! Sit down, Higgins, before you do more damage to the English language! It was bad enough for Wilfred Owen to be killed just before the end of the war, without you coming along and murdering his finest poem!'

Dave had never forgotten that lesson. There were others like it, though none quite that bad. A lot of his classmates had laughed when the teacher had humiliated him. They were afraid of that teacher themselves and wanted to appear to be on her side. Dave didn't consider why they'd laughed, but the sound of their laughter was engraved on his memory.

Ever since then he'd had a horror of being asked to stand up and speak in public, which was why he had such mixed feelings when Bill invited him to be his best man.

'I can't do it,' he said to Jean. He'd told Bill he would be delighted, but as the days went by, the more anxious he became, and so he went to Jean for advice. He'd decided what to do, but he needed to know how to break it to Bill without hurting his feelings. He told Jean about the English teacher, so she would understand. 'It'll be Bill and Margaret's great day,' he said, 'and I'll ruin it. It'll all be perfect, and then I'll come along and stumble over my words and everyone will snigger into their champagne and I'll never be able to face Bill and Margaret again, and I'll have to leave the rambling group, because they'll all be there and I won't want to face them either, and I'll even have to find a new church, because Margaret and Bill have so many friends in the congregation and they're bound to be at the wedding, and when they see me, they're going to think, "There's the man who spoiled poor Margaret and Bill's reception, and it had been such a lovely service, as well. You really would have thought a fifty-year-old man would have been able to manage something like that! Pathetic!"'

'Whoa, whoa!' said Jean. 'You're running away. You're running away with yourself, too! Is that teacher of yours going to be at the wedding?'

'No, of course not. She's probably dead.'

'Is anyone suddenly going to tell you, as you stand up to make your speech, that you should put your script in your pocket and speak from memory?'

'No.'

'And if you do stumble over the odd word, or miss something out, are people going to laugh at you?'

Dave hesitated. 'Probably not.'

'Of course they won't, Dave,' Jean said. 'Everyone in the rambling club loves you, and so do the people at church, and you won't be doing it for that bully of a teacher, but for Bill and Margaret, who are particularly fond of you, or Bill wouldn't have asked you to be his best man.'

'But what can I do?' Dave persisted. 'I'll mess things up, I know I will.'

'I've got a book on my shelves called *Feel the Fear and Do it Anyway*. Let's do it anyway! You get your speech written and then we'll have a practice. You're great at writing, Dave, we all know that; we've all read your pieces in the rambling club newsletters and the parish magazine. And you're brilliant at telling stories. Think how often you have us doubled up at our pub lunches, or over coffee after church. And you really like Bill and Margaret, and you and Bill go back such a long way. You won't find you're short of material. So when you've got it written, let me know and we'll borrow the key to the church hall, where the reception's going to be, and you can run through it with me, a little at a time if necessary. I'll sit there with my imaginary glass of champagne, or perhaps a real one, and you can imagine Bill and Margaret are sitting next to you, and there are lots of your friends in front of you, not just me, and we've all got broad smiles on our faces, and plenty of wine and happiness inside us, and we will laugh, be sure of that, but only because some of the stories you have to tell will be so hilarious. And then we'll have another run through, if necessary, and one just before the wedding day to make sure. And you'll be as nervous as a rabbit on the M25, but you'll do it, and you'll be brilliant and everyone will love you for it, especially Bill and Margaret, who will thank you for it for the rest of their days.'

Dave had no answer to that, except to agree to Jean's plans.

The day of the wedding came, and it rained, but that didn't matter, and of course Dave was Bill's best man, and the service was lovely and everyone was as happy as could be, and of course Dave was as nervous as a rabbit, and of course he dreaded the moment when he would be asked to stand up and give his speech, but Jean had given him a way of coping, and once he got going, the smiles on Bill's and Margaret's faces grew even broader and everyone was laughing one moment and crying the next. He had felt the fear, and done it anyway! He grinned at Jean as he sat down, and took a deep swig of his champagne, while everybody clapped.

What Dave did is called a 'behavioural experiment'. Dave did not forget or 'unlearn' his early experience; what he did was develop a new way of coping. When first asked, he was torn between his two options: listening to the messages from his earlier experiences and thus disappointing his friend, or agreeing to be best man and seeing his prediction of failure come true and spoiling everyone's day. As a result of the experiment, he still didn't find it a comfortable experience, but he was more enabled than before; he could turn down the shrill volume of his bullying teacher accompanied by the jeering classmates, and he could question the reliability of his conviction that he would fail.

If, like Dave, you can try such an experiment, then you have learnt a coping technique that you can use again and again, whenever you need it.

You can . . .

Disconfirm your beliefs and predictions by use of behavioural experiments.

So let's talk about an experiment. Before we move to the first part of the experiment, it will be preferable for you to be on your own, able to think reflectively about the questions asked, and able to write some things down.

Think first about a specific situation that makes you anxious. By 'anxious' we do not mean something where your anxiety is so intense that you will not entertain doing it under any circumstance, or, if you can't get out of it, you will experience profound distress. That would be to do with a genuine phobia, and is beyond the remit of this book. We mean an event where you would really rather not be there. For example, one of us very happily rides a motorcycle, but the other would much rather be on a bicycle. When one of us reads in public the words can sound fluent and full of emotion and expression; for the other reading out loud is an intensely uncomfortable and miserable experience. In other words, doing the thing we are anxious about is unpleasant, and if we can we avoid it.

Almost all of us have something in our lives that this can apply to. We would like you to describe your own event on a piece of paper, or write it into a document on your computer or tablet: an event you have avoided, or in doing it have felt uncomfortable and anxious. Now give it a name. Make sure that it can be kept secret, away from prying eyes; we want you to be a bit brutal in your honesty about your own experiences. Keep your account brief; it is only an aide-memoire, meant to help you recall your own memories.

Then try to give it a rating on a scale of 1 to 10 (where 10 is bad). This is called a SUD rating (Subject Unit of Distress). Think about the named event and remember when it was at its worst, when you felt as bad as you ever have in respect of that particular circumstance, and give that memory a rating of 10. Next, think of a time when although it was there, it didn't trouble you too much, but you were aware of it; give that a 1. From now on, any time you encounter the event you can give it your own score between 1 and 10.

Part of the function of the experiment is to see if you can get your score lower in specific situations.

So we move to the coaching stage.

Coaching

Think of and visualize the most recent time the named event happened and caused you some distress. Write down the situation or surroundings you were in, and could be in again: for example, speaking up in a meeting rather than sitting quiet when you have strong views about what is being discussed, or going for a job interview, or asking someone for help.

You are now going to think through your situation from four perspectives – the Four Buttons. This is our starting point.

First, think about how you behaved in response to that situation. Did you talk more than usual (begin to chatter), did you fall silent, did you get restless and fidgety, did you become noticeably still and try to hide away? Did your behaviour make you uncomfortable? If so, write it down in a few words, and give it a SUD rating between 1 and 10.

Second, recall how you were feeling physically in the situation. This is different from emotional feelings. We are talking about physical sensations; for example, was your stomach churning (butterflies), were your palms sweating, did your mouth go dry, were you aware of your heart pounding, or your breathing altering? If the physical sensation was uncomfortable, write it down, and give it a SUD rating between 1 and 10.

Third, what were you thinking? Try especially to identify the thoughts of that absolute, black-and-white character we referred to earlier in the chapter. It is important to try to differentiate between thoughts and feelings. As a general rule, thoughts are about events; they are interpretations and perceptions of the world in which we live. Emotions are different and have 'feeling' words to describe them. You don't *think* fear or pleasure for something or someone; you have thoughts about the thing or person that lead to you having feelings of fear or pleasure. As we discussed before, absolute, imperative and judgemental thinking language can start a vicious circle and make matters worse. How far was your thinking starting to spin that circle? Give that a SUD rating between 1 and 10.

Last, how were you feeling emotionally? Was it fear and dread, a sense of panic, frustration, anger? A fear of loss, shame and humiliation? Or maybe anticipatory excitement. Even if these feelings seemed all mixed up, try to name and identify them, and, if they were causing discomfort, give them a SUD rating between 1 and 10.

Having established our starting point, let us move on to thinking about making a difference.

Generally, there are three ways to make a difference and cope. You are invited to try them and experiment with which works best for you.

The first way is **avoidance**: put simply, not doing the thing you want to do because doing so makes you anxious. So if you are anxious about meeting other people, you turn down invitations to social events, or you accept but don't turn up. You often then end up thinking you are stupid and feeling ashamed. You don't apply for jobs, not because you can't do them but because you can't face the interview. You don't volunteer to do things, not because you are incapable but because you are afraid that if you don't get it right you will be criticized. Sometimes our avoidance involves taking comforting substances, usually food, drink or pills. Most of these avoidances result in our having negative thoughts about ourselves and feeling mixtures of guilt, shame, defeat and embarrassment.

The second means of coping is **to do it**, the 'feel the fear and do it anyway' approach. Let us explain first how it works. Think back to the example of Ken stepping into the path of a bus and being pulled from oblivion by Trevor. Neither had time to think about what to do once they had become aware of the threat from the bus. High levels of hormones were almost instantly released into their systems. But once the task was completed the levels automatically reduced; if that had not happened, Ken and Trevor would have been on a state of maximum alert for the rest of their lives, which would have been intolerable. In fact, a few minutes after the event both felt a bit flat, like damp rags. This is true of any anxiety-provoking event. We perceive something as a threat, we respond with flight and fight (which has a large physiological component), and once the catastrophe we anticipated has not occurred, our hormone levels decline and so do our anxious feelings. In time we often develop a strange familiarity with the threat and in due course our responses may become less governed by flight and fight. We don't like it, it's still disagreeable, but our estimation of the threat and catastrophe become more realistic and evidence-based, and we begin to develop coping strategies.

Now think again about the event you wrote down, and draw seven lines, numbering them 1 to 7. On line 1 write how you behave now when the event happens. On line 7 write how you would like to behave if your response was not a problem. Consider each line 2–6 to be a gradual step taking you from 1 to 7, and write on each one a small step towards your goal.

The following may illustrate what we mean. We once knew someone who had had a very bad experience at his place of employment; the consequence was that he was signed off work by his GP with debilitating anxiety. Although he did not particularly like the idea, he knew he needed to go back to work. Returning to work was part of the problem: the entrapment that made the anxiety worse. His job used the only skills he had been trained for, so alternative employment was, as far as he saw it, impossible. He was too young to retire, so was between a rock and a hard place, which itself provoked more anxiety. As part of our work together we agreed a plan of action. It might have seemed very undesirable, but we agreed that in the long term it was the most feasible. Returning to work became a goal. If this goal was not attained, we would think again. The person concerned wrote down his seven lines.

Line 1: If I need to move around the area, I do a detour
to avoid any sight of the place of work, because it is
so upsetting.

Line 2: Drive past the building when no one is around.

Line 3: Park within sight of, and facing the building, when
no one is around, and stay there for 20 minutes. Even if
the anxiety levels drop, stay where I am for 20 minutes.

Line 4: When no one is about, get out of the car and
walk about, in and around the building, for 15 minutes.
(He had a key.)

Line 5: Same as Line 4, but this time arrange to meet
someone connected with work, who is reasonably
friendly towards me, and talk together for perhaps
15 minutes.

Line 6: As line 4, but this time talk to several people, and
if I stay longer than 15 minutes, so be it. Also visit the
part of the building that is most associated with feeling
anxious and stay there for another 20 minutes.

Line 7: Return to work, gradually at first, but building up
to normal time over two or three weeks.

In that way the person concerned tested the hypothesis that
he could not cope, that the threat was too great to bear, and
the catastrophe would overwhelm him, and found that his
predictions were not as absolute as he had assumed. Yes, it
was difficult and a bit uncomfortable, but it got better. The
secretion of the hormones, and other chemicals, associated with
anxiety subsided as he got used to being back. He never forgot
the original situation; he did not unlearn the experience. Rather
he found ways of coping; he disconfirmed his prediction by
the use of his experiment.

The third means to tackle the problem is through thinking: a **cognitive approach**. Essentially this means testing the
evidence. If you remember, we discussed earlier in the book
the idea that our perceptions can be so habitual that they are

like beliefs. So perceptions and thinking processes become so quick they seem instinctive; as fast as blinking if an object is about to hit your eye. But the reality is that unlike reflexes they are in fact learnt (or conditioned) from our experience. This is one of the great discoveries made by Pavlov in the early 1900s. In his experiments he observed that dogs salivated at the sight of food. If he rang a bell simultaneously with the offering of food to the dogs, after a short while they began to salivate at the sound of the bell. Salivating is a reflex; but reflexes are not just internal and automatic, they can be learnt and conditioned by external events. Clearly in the case of Pavlov's dogs the bell was not food, but over the course of the experiment the external event became paired with food. So it is with our reactions. We can reflect on our reflex reactions and thoughts when we are anxious about an event, and check how accurate and proportionate they are. Being pulled back from the path of the bus by one's friend and feeling like a washed-out rag afterwards is fine, because there is plenty of evidence that being hit by buses is not good for us. Being anxious about loss of faith for someone doing theology is different and can be tested, as we have seen. Sure, some people who study theology lose their faith and walk away from God; others go on in their faith and perhaps help lots of people both become and grow as citizens of the kingdom of God. If the mother described at the beginning of this chapter had considered the evidence that supported her fears, she would have seen that what she assumed was inevitable was in fact merely possible and therefore much less of a threat.

The key warning words and thoughts that we need to be aware of are 'I must', 'I should', 'I ought', I've got to', 'I can't stand it' and their like – our old friends the absolute, imperative and judgemental thoughts. Cognitively checking their veracity does not remove them, or neutralize the process. But it does provide an opportunity to confirm that the thoughts and assessment of the threat and catastrophe are supported by evidence, to the extent that they can be used as a reliable predictor of what will happen.

To return to the experiment. You have identified the event and noted it down; you have also made notes on each of the Four Button responses and their SUD ratings. Now we would like you to choose which of the three coping techniques you would like to use in your experiment.

You can **avoid**, which may bring about immediate reduction in SUD but doesn't really change anything in terms of the quality of your life. It may make it worse.

You can **face up** to the feared event, object or person, and gradually test out your hypothesis that they present a threat; or you can do it all in one go.

You can **look at the evidence** that your thoughts, memories and predictions are accurate and good predictors, just as Dave was helped to do in considering the level of similarity between those listening to his best man's speech and the teacher and class in his early experience in school.

At this point, just reading about your anxiety ceases to be of much use; you now have to try the experiment and see what works. By 'works' we mean it helps you to question and reassess your estimate of the threat and of the catastrophe. It also means you will be less distressed when you encounter again the event, person or situation that previously provoked your anxiety. This does not mean you will not feel anxiety, but you will have developed ways and means of coping or managing it. It's a bit like learning the piano. You can have all the knowledge in the world about the instrument, but there's no music until you press the keys. Central is the concept of the Four Buttons: they all interlink, so any change in one produces a change in all the others.

It will be helpful to return for a moment to the story of Dave and his making the best man's speech, and analyse it from the perspective of the Four Buttons and coaching in coping. When Bill asked him to be his best man, one **thought** Dave had was,

'What an honour!' then, almost simultaneously, 'I can't do that. I know I'll make a fool of myself.' Both were so fast they were almost reflexes. The **physical** sensations he got were a sinking and tightening in his stomach and a slight increase in his heart rate. These were sparked off by the **emotional** feelings of fear and shame and his anticipating panic when it came to giving the speech. His **behaviour** was to look away, and try to find a way out of what he perceived as his predicament. But Dave did not avoid and run away. By talking it over with Jean he began to think about it differently. Jean did not advise him, but simply pointed out the evidence. Then she suggested to Dave that he could reconsider what he believed were facts gleaned from his experiences. He could experiment with different ways of thinking about himself, his experience, and what he really wanted to do, which was to be Bill's best man. She then helped with the second part of the experiment by offering support while he practised his behaviour of making his speech.

Two postscripts

First, over the past 50 years there has been a large amount of research on effective ways of helping people whose lives are adversely affected by anxiety. Remember, we are talking here about anxiety as a difficulty in day-to-day living, more of a discomfort that nags at your sense of worth, something that interferes with living the abundant life God wants for you, not a mental health problem. *If you think you have a mental health problem, your best course may be to seek help from someone qualified to first assess and describe your difficulty, and second to offer evidence-based treatment.* Your GP may offer medication. If that is the case, ask your GP what the downside of this medication might be, as well as its benefits. Your GP may also suggest you work with a therapist. Always check with your GP first, and never be reticent about asking the therapist what approach (method of therapy) will be used, and what evidence there is that it will help you. That way you will engage in the therapy more positively, and therefore will be more likely to have a beneficial outcome.

Second, there are two famous stories in the Gospels of Jesus walking on the dark waters of the Sea of Galilee and calming its sudden and furious storm. The stories are twins of one another, and draw upon the same ancient myth of God taming the forces of evil and chaos. In both of them the sea represents those forces, standing for all that might seem to overwhelm us and destroy. In numerous passages in the Old Testament we learn that there is one, and only one, who has the measure of these forces and the mastery over them, only one who can 'rule the raging of the sea' (Psalm 89.9) or 'trample the sea monster's back' (Job 9.8, GNB), and that one is God.

The stories of Jesus walking on the water and calming the storm bear witness not to the disciples seeing Jesus perform two extraordinary magic tricks on the Sea of Galilee (that is to take them too literally), but to their encountering Jesus in the deep mystery of his resurrection. With the risen Jesus they found themselves in the very heart of God, able to declare with Thomas, 'My Lord and my God!' After the brutality of the crucifixion and their own devastating sense of loss, they discovered in the risen Jesus God's eternal mastery over the forces of chaos and evil, and the impact of that discovery never left them.

Trevor once wrote a meditation on Mark's version of the calming of the storm, and delivered it as the sermon one Sunday in the Cathedral in Chester. It ended with these words:

> The Calming of the Storm is not Mark's final word.
> His God must go to Gethsemane
> to pour out his soul,
> go on and on to Golgotha
> to spend his body and his blood.
> He has the mastery,
> yet still it costs him dear.
> He has no easy victory.

Nor, too often, do we.
Yet still, still we have God with us in the boat,
even if we only half recognize him,
or think he is asleep and does not care.
And he has, he has, he has the mastery!
A man of our own times,
his faith purified in the furnace of apartheid,
wincing as a small boy at the daily humiliations his father
    had to bear,
bearing them himself as a man of the wrong colour,
listening to story after story after story of most fearful
    cruelties,
still can say with all his might
'love is stronger than hate,
life is stronger than death,
light is stronger than darkness,
and laughter, joy, compassion, gentleness and truth
are so much stronger than their ghastly counterparts'.
He and Mark join hands,
Desmond Tutu and that ancient storyteller, who knew his
    Psalms so well,
and in the light of resurrection dance the dance of truth,
laugh the laughter of heaven.

And we, we have more faith than we know,
more hope than we can understand.
How can that not be so,
when God is with us in the boat?[13]

6

'Even the hairs of your head are all counted': worry

For some people, what we said earlier in the book about anxiety may ring true, but not to the extent that it constitutes a problem. They may sometimes feel uncomfortably anxious, but for them there's a more enduring, non-specific anxiety. It's not a response to particular events or circumstances, real or perceived. It's something that hangs around, is always there. It can even seem to be part of their personality. We will call it worry.

Worry and anxiety are often understood as the same thing. For the translators of Matthew's Gospel they are the same too. In the last chapter we referred to the Revised Standard Version when we quoted Jesus saying 'do not be anxious'. Most translations made since then, including the NRSV, the NIV, the Jerusalem Bible and the New Jerusalem Bible, and the Good News Bible, have 'do not worry'. Modern psychologists, however, make some important distinctions between the two. Worry tends to be less specific, less focused on particular events or on perceptions and anticipations of such events. With worry, the overestimation of the threat and of the ensuing catastrophe, which are marks of unhelpful anxiety, are vaguer and less distinct. So while the oncoming double-decker bus or the prospect of making a speech may still be discomforting, the direct connect is not the same. Worry is something more general, more of a state of being or habit we can get into. Observing this distinction, we decided that the RSV's 'do not be anxious' was a more accurate translation of the Greek, since that passage of the Sermon on the Mount is concerned with specific things: finding enough to eat or drink, and clothes to put on one's back. (Our choice did mean we had to cheat at one point. When we quoted Matthew 6.27, 'Can any of you by being anxious add a single hour to your span of life?' we were combining the RSV with the NRSV, for the simple reason that the RSV makes a complete mess of the rest of the verse. It talks of someone adding a cubit to their span of life. We can't for the life of us see what sense you can make out of that!)

Maybe you are known, or you label yourself, as 'a bit of a worrier'. If that is the case, you will know full well that your worry is not an agent of PEACE; it is more likely to disrupt harmony and concord. Yet paradoxically you might well see your worrying as having virtues and positive functions.

> 'If I worry, it shows I care, and that the people or events I am worrying about matter to me.'

> 'If I worry, it reduces the chances of bad things happening.'

> 'I worry to ensure that I am energized, ready, prepared and committed when the time comes. I worry so that I won't be found wanting or failing at the crucial moment.'

We see here some examples of what might motivate us to worry. Yet while the objectives seem commendable, the consequences of the worry are an unease and discomfort that seem to mimic those of anxiety. There is a further paradox: although people who worry half believe their worry is a good thing, the discomfort they experience can become intrusive, and so they develop a second stage of worry: worrying about worrying. This is typified by thoughts such as:

> 'This worry is so uncomfortable, it must be doing me harm.'

> 'Being a worrier is part of who I am. I can't help it, even though I know it's not good for me.'

For us Christians this can be made much worse if we're told that worry is a sign we don't believe firmly enough in God and his love for us, or if we're encouraged to take to heart that passage in the Sermon on the Mount and we turn to one of the more contemporary translations and find we are told over and over 'not to worry'. (We won't say any more about that passage here. As we have explained, it belongs more to the discussion of anxiety.) If we are not careful, we can conclude that despite our worries having good intentions and worthy objectives, they are essentially sinful. We then end up thinking we're sinners for engaging in something we think we can't help. What a position to be in! Who'd be a Christian! 'Peace be with you.' What a joke!

When someone says, 'Don't worry, it'll all turn out right in the end,' those words are not only unhelpful, they are actually hurtful. For one thing they demonstrate a certain lack of empathy. As we have seen, people often worry because it seems to work, so the person doing the worrying is being told to abandon a coping strategy that as far as he or she can see has a good and proper purpose. And then the assurance, 'It'll all turn out right in the end,' invites the simple riposte, 'How do you know?', to which, of course, there can be no answer.

The problem about worrying is caught in that simple phrase 'coping strategy'. We worry something bad will happen, even if in all probability it won't. Then, when the bad thing doesn't happen, we say to ourselves, 'Well, I was right to worry, wasn't I?'

A friend of ours had a teenage son who had just passed his driving test. Like many young men he asked to borrow the family car to see his friends. His mum worried about that, especially if the journey involved motorways. This worrying did not come over her just when he went out in the car, but became a constant intrusion and distraction. It went round and round in her head, loaded with 'what ifs'. This was despite two facts: first, she had been in the car with him when he was learning to drive and knew he was not a headstrong risk-taker; second, injuries per mile are significantly lower on motorways than on ordinary roads. She knew that, too. She didn't tell anyone of her worry because she thought it might be dismissed as silly. But to her it was simply what caring mums do. And it worked! Every time her son used the car, he came back fit and well with an undamaged car.

Notice there is an element of this mum's worry that takes it beyond just care. It was a 'constant intrusion and distraction' and it 'went round and round in her head'. She was paying a heavy price. These are typical features of distressing worry. It distracts us when we are trying to concentrate, it intrudes when we want to do something like enjoying music or going to sleep. It produces its own troublesome ruminations: our thoughts go round and round in a circle, and end up where they started.

The question is, then, what can we do about it? We can use PEACE.

Try giving yourself **permission** to worry. After all, it's what most people do from time to time. Whether worry really is a problem for you or not is for you to decide. It's not about diagnosis by an expert or third party, it's about whether you find yourself saying, 'This troubles me, and I would like to do something about it.' Taking care about making a decision to move to another job, or worrying about your child going to a new school, is perfectly appropriate. It only becomes something else when it goes on for a disproportionate length of time, when it gets in the way of your living your life, or when it causes you agitation and distress. Worrying is not evidence of your failure as a human being or as a follower of Jesus; it's what human beings do from time to time.

Having given ourselves permission, and hopefully found some sense of proportion, we need to move on to **explanation**. For the individual, distressing worry is complex. We hope that some of the comments above will help you to recognize some of the components of worry and how they might interact. Understanding the subject, or demystifying it, frequently makes coping more manageable. In Chester Cathedral Refectory there is a large stained-glass window which was installed for the new millennium. The first response of some visitors is to say they don't like it. When they are told about the artist, however, and about what the shapes in her window symbolize and how they interact, their reaction often becomes, 'Wow! That's great!' We are not expecting readers to exclaim, 'Wow! That's great!' about their worrying, but understanding it better may move them on from, 'I can't help it; it's my lot in life to worry,' to, 'This is a bit of a problem; let's see if I can do anything about it.'

Now for **acceptance** and/or **adjustment**. It may be that you are quite happy to be a bit of a worrier; it's part of who you are, and you can live with it. However, perhaps you are getting a bit of criticism for being like that. For you the answer might be that changing is too much of a risk and too much trouble. 'This is the way God made me, and so be it.' Accepting rather than being concerned about what others think you should be might be right for you. If you would like to adjust and do things differently, though, change is always possible.

So under **coaching** we can try an experiment to see what happens to your distress from worrying. Three simple but important things need sorting out first.

1 Find a quiet space where you will not be disturbed, and put aside 15 to 20 minutes each day for the first week of the experiment, then a shorter time for some weeks after that. That time should be at least two hours before you go to bed. Try to make it the same time and place for each day.
2 Make an itemized list of the things you worry about. You don't need to go into any detail. Just make the items one or two words. You only need a quick reminder – you will have rehearsed these worries for so long, your memory will look after the rest. It will look a bit like a short shopping list.
3 Find a simple, short, pleasurable task that engages you both physically and mentally, that can quickly and easily occupy your attention.

This is called a Worry Period Experiment. It addresses the thought, 'I need to worry, or something bad will happen.' Having decided on your time and place and written your list, set a timer or alarm clock for 15 or 20 minutes, sit down, read your list and worry about its items. That way the 'necessity' of worrying will have been taken care of.

A problem may well remain, however. We are very likely to have the worry thoughts outside our 'worry period'. We know our thoughts can become like a circular script, and once they get started they can go round and round in our heads. The subjects of our worry may well come up during the day, unexpected and uninvited. If that is the case, when you think about any of the items on your list during the remaining 23½ hours, you can say to yourself, 'I don't need to worry about that now; it can wait till my worry period tomorrow.' Then, as soon as possible, engage in your simple, short, pleasurable task as a distraction. Stay with the 15–20 minute worry period for the first week, but if after that you find you are getting out of the habit of worrying, make it shorter.

Last, do an **evaluation** of what works. If you find you are worrying less and your worry is less distressing, that is good. If it has not worked as you had hoped, try devising other experiments for yourself.

For example, one experiment is to take your worries out of you and place them where someone else can look after them. You can write them down and put them aside somewhere. Or you can weave them into a prayer, and pray it out loud to God. The prayer doesn't have to be beautifully crafted; it just needs to be honest, as straightforward as you can make it. God wants us, after all, to pray to him as we are, not as perfect people, completely sorted. The Psalms are packed full of people who are not completely sorted.

Another experiment is to test your worry. Is there sound evidence that supports the idea that your worrying either causes something to happen or prevents something from happening?

If there isn't any, you can experiment with saying to yourself, 'There's no need to worry, because I know from my evidence that . . .' Then turn to a distraction. Evaluation is about confirming what works for you and using it.

And always remember, despite what some people may say, you never have to worry about God! In Matthew's Gospel, a few chapters beyond the Sermon on the Mount, we find Jesus saying this: 'Are not two sparrows sold for a penny? Yet not one of them will fall to the ground unperceived by your Father. And even the hairs of your head are all counted' (10.29–30). In the Roman world sparrows were the cheapest living things used for food, and yet, whenever a sparrow dies, Jesus is saying, God takes note. God doesn't value things according to the price people put on them. Sparrows are his creatures, and therefore his concern: the objects of his care, his compassion and love. He is *their* Father, too. And as for us human beings, God keeps a tally of the number of hairs on our heads – and it makes no difference if we are completely bald! That verse 30, just ten words long in Matthew's Greek, holds in its small compass almost everything we need to know about God's love and care for us. If *that* were to go round and round in our heads, just think what effect it might have on us! So there's another experiment for you to try, perhaps. 'Even the hairs of your head are all counted.' Repeat those words to yourself, slowly, over and over. Hear God saying them to you. Put them deep into your prayer, and into your heads. Let them pop up all over the place, as you are going for a walk, or boiling the kettle for a cup of tea. Let them play in your mind, let them play to their heart's content! (We are speaking, of course, of the heart of God.)

7

'But I am a worm': self-esteem

------◆•◆------

An untimely death

Ken was born towards the end of the 1939–45 war in Europe – to be precise, seven days before D Day. On Tuesday 23 September 1947 an event occurred that has had a significant influence on the rest of his life: his dad, Ron, died. As a young woman Ken's mum, Vera, had not considered marriage to be part of her life plan. A lot of persuading and wooing on the part of Ron had been required to get her into the church and promise to be his wife. In April 1942 he finally succeeded. Among Ron's obstacles had been Vera's thoughts and feelings about men. These had generally been negative and suspicious, a consequence of her early experiences as she was growing up. She had, to that point, seen her life as being that of a single, independent, professional nurse. In those times, when women got married they were expected to give up work, and when she became a Baptist minister's wife, Vera did just that. Having never envisaged becoming either a wife or a parent, in that dreadful September of 1947, before the advent of state welfare provision in 1948, she suddenly became a widow with a small boy to look after. Whether or not she resented him Ken cannot say or remember, but she sometimes spoke, years later, of her bewilderment, hopelessness and sheer unpreparedness for the events that had happened. What we can say, without any dispute, is that the person Ken is today is not the same one as would have existed if the events of that September Tuesday had not occurred. The memories have inevitably remained an unhappy part of his life.

They have not totally defined it – that is very far from being the case – but they have influenced him psychologically, socially, neurologically and emotionally, for they became one of the defining factors in how he saw himself and the people around him.

'Love your neighbour as yourself'

Self-esteem is a very broad concept. It is what gives us a sense of perspective and determines how we see our place in the world. It is the appraisal we make about ourselves and our projection as to what we think other people think about us, our evaluation about ourselves as individuals. That evaluation can be affected by our age, gender, sexuality or nationality; by the area and community in which we live; by the job we do and how well we do it, or by how we view our retirement; by whether the job we do or did was one we are proud of, ashamed of, or ambiguous about; by whether we are employed or unemployed; by the hobbies or activities we take part in; by achievement in the arts or sport; by the qualities we perceive in ourselves – whether we see ourselves as kind, competitive, elegant, determined, ambitious, honest, reliable, aggressive . . . ; by our faith and religious practice; even by the pets we may have, especially if they are animals that are attached to us and show us affection.

We could add many things to that list, but our self-esteem is formed also by the answers we give to some more fundamental questions. Are we loved? Do we love? Are we lovable? Are we capable of being loved and of being lovable? The answers we give may vary according to our circumstances, but they have a particular importance for Christians. For does not the book of Leviticus in the Old Testament say, 'You shall love your neighbour *as yourself*,' and does not Jesus in the Gospels of Mark, Matthew and Luke give those words a central place in his teaching, second only to those about loving God with all our heart, soul, strength and mind?

As we suggested in the opening chapter, Leviticus appears to assume we put a high value on ourselves. If we do, then we are right, for we are made 'in the image and likeness of God', as Genesis 1 would have it, and that means, as again we made plain in that first chapter, that we are 'kings' and 'queens' on his fine earth, and that we have that royal status simply through being born as human beings, an inalienable gift from our Creator.

And yet we don't feel like kings or queens most of the time. We may claim that those words from Genesis 1 are magnificent (which they are), but we don't really believe them, or we don't feel them to be true, not of us anyway. A prerequisite of love is the holding of the object of one's love in high esteem. Why is loving ourselves so elusive?

Memories, memories

Most Christians, unless they are Quakers, say the Lord's Prayer every time they gather for worship; and unless they are new to churchgoing they do not need to follow the words on the service sheet. Many of us are familiar with the creeds, or with the great faith-affirming hymns of writers such as Wesley, Townsend or Kendrick. We have said the creeds or sung those hymns so many times, we know them off by heart; they are embedded in our memories.

Understanding memory is one of the great adventures of neuroscience and psychology. At this stage in the twenty-first century we are not far beyond its beginning. What we know, so far, is that memory has many different levels of activity. For example, there is short-term memory. We are given someone's telephone number, we ring them and have a conversation; ten minutes later we think of something else we wanted to ask them, and then regret we didn't write the number down. For the life of us we can't remember what it was. An example of a different level is long-term memory. Some long-term memories are formed as a result of frequent repetition. One of us can remember *pi* (π) to four decimal places, having used it a lot in an earlier career. (The other can't remember it at all, never having made use of it since he left school.) Others are attached to events that might seem trivial but which belong to our past and to the stories we have told over the years, such as the names of pets we used to have, or the make of car our parents owned.

The memories we have about how we experienced the people around us are the ones that most profoundly influence our beliefs about ourselves. They help establish how we think about ourselves, the world we once lived in and the one we live in now. The importance and significance of these memories is widely accepted in psychology; they are among the building blocks of the people we become. Accessing them and addressing what to do with them is more controversial, but these controversies lie within and between the various schools of psychology and are not the subject of this book. Almost all psychologists accept that while we cannot obliterate them, or totally forget them, we can accommodate them and learn to live with them, in much the same way as people get used to being short. The memories are part of us and cannot be expunged, any more than the past can be undone, or a cubit added to our stature (as the King James Bible wrongly, but memorably, translates Matthew 6.27 and Luke 12.25). Wanting to change what cannot be changed is pointless and will make us unhappy. The authors of this book might have grown up passionately wanting to dance for the Royal Ballet, but as one of us didn't have the necessary physical attributes and the other was notorious in his family for his lack of dancing skills, it would have been silly to have clung to that ambition and we would only have become miserable as a result. Our early experiences of those around us and our memories of them are part of the weft and warp of the making of us, and there is nothing we can do about that. What we make of them, however, or what God makes of them, is another matter.

Such memories are sometimes called our 'schema': the ways and structures we have of organizing the information our brain is processing. Events quite beyond our control can influence our schema. Ken would not be the person he is today if his father had lived and influenced him beyond the age of three. What and how he would have been is futile speculation; we have no way of knowing. Yet it remains true that in day-to-day living schemas range in their usefulness and functionality. Unhelpful ones are sometimes called 'dysfunctional assumptions', or 'dysfunctional core beliefs'. These may resemble thoughts we have, but they differ from them in some important respects.

Thoughts versus core beliefs

Thoughts are about processing everyday events, choosing an item on a menu, deciding if we can afford to buy something or where to go on holiday, working out how to pay off our overdraft. All but the last of these may sound somewhat trivial examples, but thoughts are also involved in altogether more complex and personal situations, such as our writing this book: 'we'll structure this chapter this way or that; we hope people like what we've written; if they don't, we'll look right idiots.'

That last, 'if they don't, we'll look right idiots', is an example of what we may think, especially in stressful circumstances that provoke a certain anxiety or fear. We can mix up thinking about a task with thinking of a more personal nature – 'we'll structure this chapter this way or that; we hope people like what we've written' (task) – and conflate it with reflective or personal evaluation thinking – 'if they don't, we'll look right idiots'. From there we may go on to arrive at some very negative judgements about ourselves: 'and if we look like idiots, we *will* be idiots, useless, worthless!' Such a line of thinking and its conclusion would be driven by unachievable perfectionism. Furthermore, in being dependent on being seen by others as successful, we are risking the danger of handing over our well-being to the opinions of others.

Core beliefs, on the other hand, are more structural. Imagine that you need glasses to read this, and you have got them from an optician who has muddled up his orders, so that the lenses made for you don't match those on your prescription. Or suppose, further – to enter the realm of the absurd – the lenses you have received distort the image so much and so cleverly that the words your brain sees on the page are different from those we have written. Our perception of ourselves and other people can become similarly distorted. If, in our formative years, when our brain is growing and our sense of self is developing, we experience the world as hostile, angry and abusive, we still have to make sense of it and our reasoning may go something like this: 'The world I am experiencing is not nice and sometimes actually hurts. I am dependent on this world to feed, clothe and protect me; so if I protest, I am putting myself at risk. Better play safe and blame me.'

So children who experience hostility grow up anxious, not knowing how to trust; children who experience persistent unkindness believe they are worthless; children who frequently experience anger grow up with a sense that everything they do is wrong and that they are guilty; children who experience abuse believe, when they are adults, that they are the lowest of the low.

Yet that is not the whole story; other chapters in our lives come to be written. In Vera's case her discomfort with men was certainly part of her story, a significant part of her schema. We don't know, nor probably ever will know, what led to her distrust. But we can observe that her brief years with Ron brought her a different perspective. She never fully forgot her earlier experiences, the ones that had marked her before she met him, but she did learn to live with them, to the point where she was able to be more content and live happily as a minister's wife. The schema they established lasted for the whole of her life, yet from Tuesday 23 September 1947 until the day she died in 2000 her happiness with Ron belonged firmly to her memory, and played its own part in making her the person she was.

Room for God's remaking: two stories from the Gospels

To suggest we are simply the product of our early experiences, especially our bad ones, is to give in to a lazy determinism that robs us of our dignity, our freedom and our responsibility, and leaves no room for hope, or for grace and God's remaking. For children whose experiences were damaging, the hostile, the unkind, the angry and the abusive need not continue to win throughout the rest of their lives. The Gospels are full of stories of fractured people encountering Jesus and being profoundly changed as a result.

Apart from the stories of Jesus raising someone from the dead, perhaps the most extreme example of change is that in one who calls himself Legion, the man found by Jesus living among tombs beside the Sea of Galilee. The story is given to us by Matthew, Mark and Luke, and the earliest of those versions is Mark's (5.1–20). Why does the man give himself such a name, Legion? It isn't the name his parents gave him when he was born. 'My name is Legion; for we are many,' he tells Jesus. The poor man believes that a vast horde of demons have set up home within him. But why *Legion*? Why that name in particular? In Mark's world legion meant only one thing: a division of Roman soldiers. If we return to the original Greek of his chapter 5, we discover that it has other military terms besides. There is an *agele* of pigs. Translators often render that as 'herd', but pigs don't really go around in herds. *Agele* was, in fact, often used of a band of military recruits. Jesus 'dismisses' the demons, so that they enter the pigs, and 'dismisses' reminds us, as it would have reminded Mark's readers, of a military command. The pigs 'charge' into the lake, like troops rushing into battle.

Mark's writing can seem so simple, but every word is carefully chosen here. Is he suggesting that the man who calls himself Legion had been caught up in the horrors of war?

Josephus, the first-century Jewish historian, gives us an account of a Roman legion recapturing the exact area where Mark's story is set. He describes events that happened some years after Jesus of Nazareth, but they might well have been in Mark's mind as he wrote the story in the precise way he did. Josephus speaks of mass slaughter in one particular town, families captured, property plundered, houses set on fire. Then, he continues, they 'marched against the surrounding villages. Those who were able-bodied fled, the weak perished, and all that was left went up in flames.'[14] (It could, alas, be describing too many areas in our contemporary world, including Iraq, or Syria.) Had Legion been in the midst of such horrors, and escaped by the skin of his teeth? Is that what Mark wants us to imagine?

Whatever the truth of the matter, his remarkable story brings us, at its start, a man among the dead, who is barely alive beyond mere existing. He is given to fearful violence against those who try to restrain him, and against himself. He breaks chains and shackles and self-harms, he howls day and night, and when Jesus approaches him he tries to drive him away with his shouting. He sees himself as utterly worthless and as quite beyond hope. Naked, he thinks he has no single shred of honour, no scrap of dignity left. His view of things is so distorted that although he recognizes Jesus as 'Son of the Most High God', he believes he can only bring him further torment, when his distress is already beyond all bearing. By the end of the story, however, this same man is sitting quietly, 'clothed and in his right mind', begging Jesus to let him follow him on his journey. 'Go home,' Jesus replies, 'and tell them how much the Lord has done for you, and what mercy he has shown you.' He restores him to his family and his community, and turns him into an evangelist!

The man's story is over too soon, of course. We don't even learn what his real name is, and he never appears again. To our ears his restoration is made to sound too easy and too quick. But that is how it is in the Gospels, how they tell things. And yet Mark has given us a dramatic (*extremely* dramatic!) example of what can happen when a broken person, even one whose damage seems quite irreparable, comes within touching distance of the incarnate Love of God.

Luke gives us a quieter but equally telling example in his story of the bent woman (Luke 13.10–17, and in no other Gospel). It begins with Jesus playing the role of a learned rabbi, for he is teaching in a synagogue on the Sabbath. Then the story continues with this:

> Just then there appeared a woman with a spirit that had crippled her for eighteen years. She was bent over and was quite unable to stand up straight. When Jesus saw her, he called her over and said, 'Woman, you are set free from your ailment.'

Women were active in ancient synagogues and sometimes played significant leadership roles, but not this woman, not when she can only see anything more than the patch of ground at her feet if she twists her neck and looks on a slant. Why is she there? Despite what the leader of the synagogue will say later in the story, there is no suggestion that she has come to be healed. It is the Sabbath and she is there to worship God with her community, as no doubt she is every week. That is the most natural conclusion to draw from Luke's writing. Whatever the case, she is a woman on the edge, literally as well as metaphorically, for Jesus, when he sees her, has to call her over.

But what exactly does Jesus see? She is enough to stop him in his tracks and interrupt his Sabbath teaching.

Trevor visited St Petersburg in Russia in 1991, when it was still called Leningrad and just the occasional beige or grey car wove its way down the streets round the deep potholes. Slowly crossing those streets or shuffling along the pavements were a number of small old women, dressed in black and bent right over like the woman in the synagogue. Whenever he hears Luke's story, Trevor thinks of those Russian women, survivors of the German siege of the Second World War and of the various bitter privations visited upon the city by Stalin.

For Megan McKenna the story reminds her of Japan:

> I noticed older men and women so stooped and bent that they were unable to stand up. They were given seats in the trains and deferred to by those who were middle-aged. But it wasn't until I travelled to the countryside that I realized these were farmers who had grown up in the rice fields, bent over and hand-sowing, weeding and reaping the rice harvest.[15]

Another American New Testament scholar, Frances Taylor Gench, makes an even more intriguing connection. She points out that if we translate Luke's Greek literally he describes the woman in 13.11 as suffering from 'a spirit of weakness'. (And in the next verse, when Jesus enables her to stand straight, he says to her, 'Woman, you are set free from your weakness.') 'Interestingly,' Gench goes on, 'we have today become increasingly aware that low self-esteem, which diminishes and deforms the lives of many young girls and women, can also be described as a spirit of weakness.'[16]

So is this what Jesus sees in that synagogue on the Sabbath, a woman whose adult life has been cruelly distorted by crippling low self-esteem? We don't know. Luke's description of her condition is too vague, but precisely because he tells us so little, we are free, within the bounds of the story, to imagine and to speculate. And if the cap fits . . .

But certain crucial things Luke does make clear. Jesus sees a devout Jewish woman who is on the edge but who belongs in the centre – that is why he calls her to him. He sees someone who needs to be able to do her own seeing without looking slant; he sees a person who has no voice and who needs to be given one – as soon as he straightens her up, she begins praising God. He sees someone who is used to being as she is, and who has no hope of being anything else – she does not approach Jesus, he has to call her to him. Yet more than that, much more than that, Jesus sees 'a daughter of Abraham whom Satan bound for eighteen long years'. Those are the words Luke has him speak near the end of the story. To call her 'a daughter of Abraham' is to accord her a singular honour. No other woman in the Bible is called that. No woman in Jewish non-biblical literature earlier than Luke, or contemporary with him, appears with that title, either.

Jesus, according to Luke, who uses the thought forms and language of the first-century Jew, sees her as 'bound by Satan'. She is, when she first catches Jesus' eye, like a prisoner in her own body, with a strong gaoler bent on keeping her weak, one who has no compassion for her, who does not even recognize her as a human being, but only means her harm and hurt. She will die in that prison. No doubt that is what she assumes, as does everyone else who knows her. But not Jesus. Jesus sees her with a burning compassion and a hope born of the fire of the Spirit of God. He sees her for what she is: a 'daughter of Abraham', no less! She has come to her synagogue for her God. Well then, let her meet him face to face! She will find more than she bargained for. She shuffles over to Jesus and he turns the key and sets her free. Did he not say, in another synagogue, that God had sent him 'to proclaim release to the captives'? (Luke 4.18).

This story also is too short. Nowhere do we learn the woman's name or where she lives; like Legion, she is a one-scener and we hear no more of her. Did she up and follow Jesus? It is quite possible, for as we learn, if we look at the Gospels care-fully, Jesus' most loyal and devoted followers were women who had been healed by him. But if she did, we are not told. She finds her voice in the synagogue, but Luke gives her no words to say. At least Mark lets us hear the voice of the man among the tombs; in Luke 13 we are left to our imaginations. Yet, although in his telling of her story Luke does not empower this woman as much as we would have liked, Jesus does. She leaves that synagogue with her head held high, and the extraordinary words 'daughter of Abraham' ringing in her ears. She will bear that honour for the rest of her life. It will be a light load.

And now her story is told to give *us* hope, to bring us into the presence of God so that we also can find our true honour, worth and dignity, and, perhaps for the first time for 18 years or more, hold our heads high.

Dysfunctional assumptions

But in Jesus' company we have run on too far and too fast. We need to return to those pesky 'dysfunctional assumptions' and examine them in more detail. We need to be able to recognize them in ourselves, so that they do not seriously impede our well-being.

They have certain invariable characteristics, though the mix differs from one individual to the next:

1 **They are always statements, never suggestions.** They leave no room for ambiguity; they are absolute. Their subject is always either you, or how you are perceived by others, often both. For example: 'You're useless. You've always been a problem and let everyone down, and, what's more, you always will.' Frequently they have that accusing tone and content.

2 **They are untrue and irrational.** Dysfunctional assumptions do not follow on from reality, nor are they supported by evidence; they are evaluative exaggerations. 'I'm a useless person. I can't stand the way I feel; I'm deeply flawed. I'm ashamed to say I'm a Christian; I'm not good enough and I let God down all the time.'

3 **They take the form of commands.** Dysfunctional assumptions are not conditional, nor relative. They contain demanding words or phrases such as 'must, 'should', 'got to', 'need to', 'ought', or thoughts such as, 'if you're any good you will ...' For example: 'I must do it perfectly; I must be a total success

or I'm a total failure. People, and God too, *must* see what a competent, good person I am.'

4 **They lead to disturbed emotions.** These are not simply strong emotions, like the response you may have if someone you love says, 'I love you'; or the effect upon you of seeing a production of *War Horse* or hearing the blues sung by Billie Holiday. We are talking about extreme, incapacitating and disabling emotions, typified by depression, anger and anxiety.

5 **They do not help to achieve what you want.** Dysfunctional assumptions are not called dysfunctional for nothing. They inhibit and disable you, and separate you from those activities that contribute to a sense of motivation, pleasure and worth. 'Contentment is for the fortunate and lucky few who are blessed by God; and that doesn't mean me.'

6 **They tend to focus on the past or the future.** 'People like you can't do that. You'll look completely stupid. Last time you tried it you got it completely wrong; you made such a mess of it that everyone who knew you was ashamed and embarrassed. Let so-and-so take it on. He's got what it takes. He doesn't want you sticking your nose in and spoiling things.'

It doesn't take much imagination to see that thoughts and beliefs such as these are not going to boost our confidence in ourselves, or enhance our capacity to live active and fulfilling lives.

These unhelpful thoughts and beliefs can be deeply ingrained in our brains. As we have said, they become part of the weft and warp of who we are. What, then, since they are such a major component of our identity, are we going to do about them?

Here we arrive once more at PEACE.

Permission

This section is very important. We will need to contradict the messages we have acquired over a long period: 'You're of no worth; there it is, put up with it, it's a fact.' Giving yourself permission means saying implicitly, if not explicitly, 'That might not be true'; it means acknowledging what you may not have admitted to yourself for a long time: 'I have, at least, *some* value and worth. I am having difficulty working with this, not because I was born with low self-esteem, but because I acquired it along the way, because it was dumped on me as I grew up.' If we are made in God's image, if we are born as an icon of God, how can we possibly come into the world with low self-esteem?

But if low self-esteem is not innate, that gives us a range of things we can do about it.

Since we are looking at permission, we are considering what are, in essence, thinking tasks. Their objective is to question the validity of the beliefs we have about ourselves that fuel our low self-esteem. They involve addressing questions about source and evidence: Where did you learn that? Is the source reliable? What is the evidence to support it?

It may help to give the example of a fictional Jane. Jane does not exist, but is a composite of some of the people we have known and worked with who held themselves in low esteem. Jane was born into a family where both parents were busy professionals. The whole family, including Jane, were active Christians and were involved in much of church life. She and her siblings were often looked after by 'uncles' and 'aunts', as she called them, from their church community. Much of the time it was great fun. There were often treats to be had and boundaries to be pushed. One day, when Jane was eight, her parents were going to be out late and a friendly couple agreed to collect the children from school and look after them over-night if necessary. It was necessary. The parents hadn't returned when Jane and her brothers needed to go to bed. She'd been lying in bed for about 15 minutes when she heard someone coming upstairs. She assumed they were just going to the toilet. She was already half asleep, but then, instead of hearing the steps going downstairs again, she realized they were coming along the landing. 'No problem,' she thought, 'they're having an early night.' But next her bedroom door quietly opened, and before she got awake enough there was someone in her bed. Befuddled thoughts of 'who? what? why?' bumped into each other, and emotions of fear and panic flooded her mind. While he did not rape her in the formal, legal sense, he certainly 'had his way with her', as the dreadful euphemism goes. After he'd finished, but still embracing her, he whispered into her ear, 'Don't tell anyone. The wife is downstairs and she hasn't heard anything, so if you don't keep quiet, she'll tell people what a liar you are. Everyone knows what a naughty girl you are. No one believes anything you say.'

Jane is now an adult, and still, remarkably you might think, an active member of the Church. Her parents, both dead, remained unaware to the end of her terrible experience. For a while afterwards they were somewhat bewildered by her behaviour. She'd suddenly become quieter and less outgoing, but eventually they explained it to themselves as just a stage she was going through in her growing up.

As well as attending church on a Sunday, Jane helps run a group for older people who have become a bit muddled. No one really notices her or her work. She just gets on with it, never makes a fuss, and if you wanted to be unkind, you might call her a bit of a mouse. When people are asked a direct question, they'll tell you she does a great job, and that the members of the club are very fond of her. They don't usually say that to Jane herself, but if they do, she doesn't believe them. Sometimes she has ideas of how things might be done better, but she never says anything. The message constantly repeats on a loop in her head: 'You may be trying to do good things, but people know what a liar you are. Everyone knows what a naughty girl you are; no one believes anything you say.'

We can now ask Jane our questions, first about her source: 'Where did you learn this message that keeps going round in your head? Who told it to you, and under what circumstances? Answer those, and then tell us whether you think it can be relied on as true.' As the hearers of this story, we can ask ourselves this: should Jane respect the man who put such ideas into her head, thus enhancing their truth, or might we think he had other reasons for wanting her not to tell anyone and to believe what a naughty person she was?

Turning back to Jane, we can go on to the question of evidence. 'What,' we can ask her, 'is the evidence in your present life that supports this belief about yourself? If you really are a congenital liar and as naughty as that man said you were, would you be working with vulnerable people and doing such a good job with them?'

The answers to these questions seem to us patently obvious, but Jane still needs to be encouraged to answer them for herself. She needs to recognize that her estimate of herself stems from one who terrified and abused her when she was just eight years old and quite unable to defend herself. The man instilled in her the ideas of her being naughty and a liar purely for his own benefit, and not because they were true. She also needs to be helped to measure the ideas against the evidence from her adult life. That evidence runs clean counter to the beliefs she has about herself, but she needs to acknowledge that to herself.

Once things have begun to sink in, she can entertain and explore the idea that she can give herself permission to start removing her abuser's power from her life. She can permit herself to discover what it's like to think of herself as truthful, reliable, loving, even good, and to think of God loving her, even delighting in her (and God cannot and never will abuse).

A leaflet was produced recently by the charity Operation Smile that tells the story of a two-year-old child called Ngan. Ngan had had a hare lip. 'Since she was born,' reads the leaflet, 'Ngan had been living in shame and isolation in a small village in southern Vietnam. Her broken smile made her an outcast, an object of revulsion. Her family thought she had been cursed. They had never seen a baby with a cleft lip and a hole in her palate before.' Her mother, however, had taken her to a clinic financed by Operation Smile, and she had been operated on by a specialist surgeon and medical team. 'After her operation,' the leaflet continues, 'Ngan looks in the mirror. Her smile is mended. Everyone is beaming. Her mother cries with happiness. A year later, on the Operation Smile follow-up visit, Ngan is transformed. She is accepted in her village, she is no longer cursed, no longer an outcast. For the first time she has friends to play with and is treated like a normal little girl.'

But in fact things will not have been quite that simple. Ngan will have continued to have memories of taunting and rejection. Her lip and palate were fixed, but she cannot have an operation to cure the way she thinks. So too with Jane. She will find it extremely difficult to change; rubbishing herself has been for too long too ingrained a habit. However, the origin of her belief about herself is now understood. Moreover, she can see it as a normal response to what happened to her. That does not make it desirable, of course, for what was done to her was and always will be a wicked thing. But no longer does she have to think of herself as a flawed person. Because of the behaviour of her abuser and the contamination of her developing brain, she has grown used to the idea of being of little worth. Her past will always be with her, but the lie has been exposed; the lie has been exposed . . . and the liar was not her! She can now experiment with the part her past will play in her future.

We need to make an important point here. The story of Jane is an example of how such negative events in our early lives can become pervasive components in how we see ourselves and can result in low self-esteem. We should not assume, of course, that everyone with low self-esteem has been sexually abused. Clearly that is not true. Nor do all who have been abused in that way necessarily have low self-esteem. Among the potential root causes of low self-esteem are separation from parents or family at critical times in someone's development; prolonged periods living in an environment where one is deprived of nurture or affection; narrow, restricted family aspirations and poverty. One of us once worked with a woman who'd been called by all the members of her family, including her mother and father, not by her own name but after a species of family pet. In adulthood, the effect of this on her self-esteem was, to say the least, debilitating.

The root causes of low self-esteem belong to a continuum that stretches from sudden, single events, such as Jane's being abused that evening, through to continuous and deliberately inflicted discomfort. Indeed, all assaults on our persona can damage our sense of who we are and our estimate of our own worth.

We are not suggesting that we should attempt to protect children from all risk, or refuse to discipline them or punish them. Children need from a very early age to learn that there are boundaries they should not cross, and that if they do, they are likely to hurt themselves or others. They need to develop their understanding of the consequences of their actions. If they don't, they will end up as selfish and thoughtless adults. They also need to learn how to handle difficult situations. Overprotect children and they will grow up reckless or insecure. Ken can recall how much he learnt about life from his apprenticeship in the motor industry in the 1960s, and how uncomfortable much of that learning was. As a mature adult he can see that the people who taught him those lessons were not trying to do him down, but rather wished him well, and wanted him to learn what mistakes can be made and their consequences. What we are talking about is attacks on the persona, on the person made in God's image, on what makes us all, in the eyes of God, holy.

With appropriate help people not only survive such attacks, even prolonged ones, but can even become stronger and more caring as a result. While Trevor was on the staff of Chester Cathedral, he and one of his daughters, Sarah, led three pilgrimages to Russia. Sarah is a Russian speaker and the Executive Secretary of St Gregory's Foundation, which works with some remarkable partner organizations in Russia and the former Soviet Union, supporting them with finance and, where appropriate, with expertise. The third pilgrimage in 2009 found us sitting in a circle on the grass of a park in St Petersburg one sunny afternoon with a group of some 12 young Russian mums and their small children. If you'd observed those young women and how they interacted with their children, you would probably have said they seemed exemplary mothers and their children were secure and clearly knew they were loved. One small boy in a pushchair was asleep when we arrived, and woke up feeling grumpy, as sometimes children do, and not at all pleased suddenly to find so many strange faces. His mum was brilliant with him, and though he cried for a time, he was soon joining in with the proceedings. All the children had made things for us in advance. They gave them to us one by one, and that little boy cheerfully handed us his present.

You would never have guessed that all those women had grown up in Russian orphanages, and that when their children were first born, many of them had not known how to establish eye contact with them, let alone speak to them or play with them. In their own formative years they had never known parental love, only the harsh regime of an institution. But they all belonged to the Sunflower Club (supported by St Gregory's), and that club had given them the companionship and support of others who shared a similar history, expert help with their parenting skills, and above all a belief in themselves and a sense of their own worth. We could see that in their eyes and in their body language. One of the leaders of the club, Masha, was sitting in the circle. She too had been brought up in an orphanage.

Never underestimate the effects of human care, sensitivity and compassion, or of the grace and unfathomable and unstoppable ingenuity of God!

Explanation

As we move along the course of PEACE from 'permission' to 'explanation', much can be deduced from what we have already said. Explanation here means emphasizing that no one is born with, or genetically inherits, low self-esteem. When we suffer from it, we can understand that it is a consequence of the behaviour of, and our relationship with, our early environment.

But we can go further than this. It used to be thought that our brains were physiologically static: their components and interconnections were developed early on, and, bar injury, remained the same throughout our lives. We now see that this view was false. Our brains interact with the circumstances in which we find ourselves throughout our lives. We keep learning and memorizing new things because our brains continue to change; they have an inherent property of plasticity.

As a general rule the younger we are, the greater our brain's plasticity. That is why our early experience is so important for our core beliefs about ourselves and others, whether that experience be positive or negative. It is not just a matter of psychology, of thinking and feelings, but of physiology, the nature of the structure of our brains. Yet still, because our brains continue to change and develop as we grow older, there is always a potential for things to be different. Hope is not an illusion! As you read this book you may be learning something new, and that is evidence of your brain's plasticity. Trevor had to learn biblical Hebrew, and quickly too, when in his late thirties, well past what you would call his formative years, he took up a post at a theological college teaching Old Testament studies. Ken's late mother-in-law learnt to drive in her mid-sixties. Like other drivers, she learnt to react in a new way to what she saw in front of her and around her, and as she became more practised these reactions seemed so natural they looked instinctive. Her brain had reformed in order to handle a bewildering array of new information without deliberate thought. And Trevor would say that reading Old Testament passages in the original Hebrew blew his mind!

Acceptance and/or adjustment

Despite what we have just said, the description of childhood and adolescence as our 'formative years' is one of those clichés which over time has come to be seen as having a secure evidence base. It is now understood that such a description refers not only to the development of our attitudes, beliefs, thoughts, emotions and feelings, but also to the very structure of our brains.

How much control and sway we have over events as adults will vary according to our age, our gender, the society and community we belong to, and our particular circumstances. But clearly children and adolescents tend to have much less control than the adults around them. Some psychological models of therapy place great emphasis on looking back into the childhood of the person who needs help. The problem with this view is that the past is just that: past. We cannot change what has happened. We may, however, with maturity and reflection, understand it differently, and this will have an impact on how we feel and on how we value our lives and ourselves.

The present and future are a different matter. So accepting that our self-esteem and sense of worth have been significantly influenced by our life experience is a matter of wisdom. Deciding to experiment with adjusting for a different future is a matter of courage and faith.

Coaching

This is the action that facilitates change; it is the section where we focus on experiments. In this chapter we are suggesting two experiments, and you can choose either or a combination of both. The objective is the same in each: for you to explore the means whereby you can begin to experience some of the abundant life God planned for you. The experiment will have worked if it tells you something and increases your knowledge.

Lots of people who want to help others advise them to change. Yet sometimes people who wish to help do not take the time to learn how those they are advising see their lives and the difficulties that go with them. Some of their suggestions may make matters worse rather than better. Just telling a person with low self-esteem how wonderful she is, and saying she just needs the confidence to get out there and do it, may make the helper feel better, but the person's internal messaging system can translate that into, 'Look how weak and pathetic I am! I can't even take helpful advice when it's offered. When they told me all those years ago I was useless, they were right, weren't they?'

We know from long experience that contradicting the negative beliefs that people with low self-esteem have about themselves is virtually pointless. What works is trying some carefully considered experiments. Two points are important: first, we need to do the experiments and discover things for ourselves, as being told the conclusion by someone else might possibly help in the short term, but the benefits are very unlikely to last. Second, we need to recognize that evidence will almost certainly emerge from the experiments to contradict the beliefs we hold about ourselves. It then becomes difficult for us to acknowledge the results of the experiment and cling to those old beliefs at the same time. But, of course, that is the point; the beliefs are shown to be false.

Pre-experiment

The objective of this is to help you to get used to the idea of observing and recording information about yourself and the patterns of your life.

Keep a diary for a week. Complete it for each day, and comment on how the day has gone for you, especially when you have thought at some point you were being put upon, or not being taken seriously, or you regret that you were not more assertive. Then try to remember what was going on just before or as you were having these thoughts, and write that down. Now comment on what you *think* about yourself, the assessment you would make of yourself, having gone through that particular experience. Last, record how you are *feeling*, with a rating of the intensity of that feeling (for example, between 1 and 10).

As with the previous exercises, you may prefer to use a chart rather than diary prose. We have given an example for Jim (see Table 7.1, overleaf).

We suggest you write your diary or chart (see Table 7.2 on p. 131 for a model you can use or photocopy it to write in) when you have finished your main tasks for the day, but allow a reasonable amount of time for it before you go to bed. You don't want to be reminding yourself of your negative thoughts just as you want to go to sleep.

Experiment

After a few days, begin to experiment.

The pre-experiment allows you to understand how you are responding to what you see as negative events that confirm your low opinion of yourself. It provides a record or description of their effect on your thinking and behaviour. As we discussed earlier, our thinking about ourselves and our behaviour can become habitual to the point that we are hardly aware of it or its contents. That is why it's so important to do the Thought record 1 exercise; it reminds us of what we are unwittingly doing.

Our memory of words we say or think is not as reliable as the words we write down. We may believe we remember what we said or thought in a particular situation, but in fact, as research has shown, our memory tends to fade quite quickly, unless we write things down and have something to refer back to. It is important, therefore, that we take the trouble to do that.

It's also useful, in column 4, to use emotional words that describe our feelings, rather than ones that talk of matters of fact or of our intentions. It is better to write about feeling 'forlorn' rather than saying, 'Nobody spoke to me today'; or about being 'angry' rather than, 'I'm going to tell him what I think.'

Table 7.1 Thought record 1 – Jim's example

Time	What is going on	What you are thinking, or the statements you are making, about yourself	How are you feeling? Rate from 1 (bad) to 10 (good)
Weds 6.00 p.m.	Got home from work, no post and no phone messages. Was hoping Carl would have been in touch about going out over the weekend.	I am not an interesting person. Nobody wants to know me. What they said when I was a child is true; it's always been like this.	Unattractive as a person and uninteresting. Not worth much. (2)
Thurs 9.00 a.m.	Important meeting at 10.00 a.m. Minutes of last meeting just arrived in emails. See my name is missed off 'Present', although I made a sizeable contribution and effort to brief myself.	My part in the meeting was of no consequence or significance. Even though I made an effort it is worthless. I am disregarded, even at work. I have got to make people take note of me.	Disregarded and of no significance. (2)

Table 7.2 Thought record 1

Time	What is going on	What you are thinking, or the statements you are making, about yourself	How are you feeling? Rate from 1 (bad) to 10 (good)

Table 7.3 Thought record 2 – Jim's example

1	2	3	4	5	6	7	8
Time	What is going on?	What you are thinking, or the statements you are making, about yourself	How are you feeling? Rate from 1 (bad) to 10 (good)	Where did I learn that thought about me from?	Evidence to support thought	What would God say about me in this situation and to this thought?	How are you feeling now? Rate from 1 (bad) to 10 (good)
Weds 6.00 p.m.	Got home from work, no post and no phone messages. Was hoping Carl would have been in touch about going out over the weekend.	I am not an interesting person. Nobody wants to know me. What they said when I was a child is true; it's always been like this.	Unattractive as a person and uninteresting. Not worth much. (2)	Mum and Dad loved me but they were almost never there, and I just wanted to be with them. I thought it was because I wasn't important enough to them, that something else mattered more. A teacher was always telling me I could do better even when I tried very hard.	Not much. Sure, I was hoping Carl would have rung but it is still only Wednesday and I know he has a big project on this week. When I left work Pat asked if I wanted to go to the match on Saturday with a group of mates. She would not have asked me if I were 'not interesting'. I can always text Carl to wish him well with the project and remind him about meeting up.	When you were born I loved you and I have loved you ever since. Nothing is insignificant to me, not even you, Jim.	Pat asking me to the match was kind; I do feel a bit more wanted and valued. (7)

| Thurs 9.00 a.m. | Important meeting at 10.00 a.m. Minutes of last meeting just arrived in emails. See my name is missed off 'Present', although I made a sizeable contribution and effort to brief myself. | My part in the meeting was of no consequence or significance. Even though I made an effort it is worthless. I am disregarded, even at work. I have got to make people take note of me. | Disregarded and of no significance. (2) | I was never a star at school, not at sport, or drama either, nor did I get any academic recognition. I had hardly any friends at school or home and because Mum and Dad were not there much I did not have 'play dates' like others in the class. I learnt to keep out of the way. I was afraid that if I had got noticed I would not know what to do and that would have been terrible and made matters worse. | Some of it is partly true; I did get missed off the attendance in the minutes, but nobody likes that. It's a mistake anyone can make and the minute taker is new to the job. There were several references in the minutes to the work I had done, also to its originality and value. | I hold the most beautiful things in my creation to be insignificant when I think about you. | Less miffed and assured that I made a contribution. A bit of satisfaction. (8) |

Experimenting with change

We are now moving on to the experimenting with change stage. Again, it is your choice whether your preference is to use a prose diary or a chart, but attention to the contents of the columns is essential in either case.

Having gathered the information about the processes involved in our low self-esteem, we can experiment with the validity of our thoughts. Write down your responses to the items at the head of each column: columns 1–4 are in essence similar to those of Record chart 1; the experimental section comes in columns 5–8. These are the responses that are designed to effect change, to give you a set of skills to modify your thinking, and to challenge, or disconfirm, beliefs you previously held to be absolutely certain. Table 7.3 (pp. 132–3) shows the example of Jim's chart. This is a particularly important section, and we need to make things as clear as we can, commenting on each column in turn.

You can use this model when you begin your experiment (see Table 7.4, which you may photocopy to write in if you choose to). The following notes on how to approach filling in your chart may provide helpful guidance.

Column 5

Having gathered the evidence in columns 1–4, the next question is, 'Where and how did you learn that?' Ask yourself, was it a matter of a sudden, single event, or was it through prolonged or repeated events? Who did you learn it from? Was it someone you respected and whose opinion you valued, or someone who was unkind and abusive, perhaps someone whose opinion on any other subject you would tend to dismiss and disregard? Or was it someone like Jim's mum, who had her own problems?

Remember, we are not born or created with negative beliefs and thoughts about ourselves. We acquire them as a result of how others treat us along the way. Our height and the colour

Table 7.4 Thought record 2

1	2	3	4	5	6	7	8
Time	What is going on?	What you are thinking, or the statements you are making, about yourself	How are you feeling? Rate from 1 (bad) to 10 (good)	Where did I learn that thought about me from?	Evidence to support thought	What would God say about me in this situation and to this thought?	How are you feeling now? Rate from 1 (bad) to 10 (good)

of our skin are aspects of us that are extremely difficult or impossible to change. But if the negative beliefs and thoughts we have about ourselves are ones we have learnt, as indeed they are, then we can learn alternatives. There is real hope for us here!

Column 6

No matter how true and valid we think events were in the past, there are always questions to be asked about how true they are now, in the present. Jim's experience of school was generally a bad one. Lacking the sporting, musical or acting talents of many of his fellow pupils, and not being articulate either, meant that when teams were selected he was frequently the one holding his head down at the bottom of the list. But as Paul put it in that famous poem in 1 Corinthians 13, 'When I was a child, I spoke like a child, I thought like a child, I reasoned like a child; but when I became an adult, I put an end to childish ways.' Jim was a man now; he had plenty of evidence that he had acquired knowledge, skills, experience and expertise, and had demonstrated commitment. The truth of his experience in his childhood was not sustainable in the face of the evidence from his adult life. He may have been missed off the attendance list in the minutes, but he did not have to interpret that in a negative way. There was considerable evidence that invited an alternative perspective.

Column 7

This column asks, what would God's response be to our scolding self-talk and beliefs? Here you have to be careful, for the way you answer the question will depend on what kind of God you believe you are dealing with. It might be helpful to look at what we have put in column 7 in Jim's example sheet, and to turn back to Chapter 3, particularly the last few paragraphs. The authors of this book do not wish to scold you or reprove you, and if we, as fallible, flawed human beings, don't want to do that, how much less will God want to! Remember what was said near the end of that chapter: 'God cannot be less forgiving, less generous, less loving than the most forgiving, the most generous, the most loving of human beings. That is a divine impossibility!'

Nevertheless, we don't want to tell you what to say here, but for you to be honest with yourself. If you sincerely believe that God *does* reprove you, or even condemns you, turns his back on you, or wishes to punish you, then write that down. But then you must recognize that your response begs further questions: How did you learn that God is like that? Who taught it to you? Were you brought up to believe in a punishing God? Is that the kind of God you hear about in the sermons in the church you attend? If you turn from what you have been taught about God to your own deepest encounters with him, might you answer the question differently? Have you ever knelt beside the Bethlehem manger and found yourself looking 'level-eyed into the face of God'? Have you ever caught sight of God running up the road to fling his arms about you, or heard him say those astonishing words, 'all that is mine is yours'? Have you ever dared to look down to find God 'washing your feet', or imagined the marks of her floury hands upon your back? Have you ever looked into the eyes of the crucified God? If this rings true, or any part of it, then dwell on that for a moment, and then see how you might complete column 7.

Column 8

What new thoughts can we have, based not on how we have always seen things, but on the evidence of our lives – the facts as they are, here and now – and on a deeper encounter with that crazy, all-encompassing love of God? In our example Jim acknowledged his mum might have had her own needs and problems, while his problems with Carl's failure to contact him were resolved by a decision to take action himself (phone on Friday). He thought again about the missing out of his name on the minutes; it was more likely to be a simple typing error than a deliberate slight against him. Certainly it had nothing to do with his experiences at school. Some of his colleagues, including the person who took the minutes and typed them up, were not even born when he was at school!

The figure you put in this column will allow you to see if the components of the experiment produced the outcome you were looking for. Has the figure changed from the one you put in column 4? If it has, and if it has moved in a positive direction, then the active ingredients of the experiment have been effective to some degree or other. If it hasn't, then providing you have learnt that you can influence your present and future, rather than be a victim of your past and what others did to you, feel free to experiment with the experiment and shape it to your particular needs. You may also find it useful to revisit Chapter 2.

Experiment variation

We have a variation on this experiment to suggest, which would give you a second bite of the cherry, so to speak, and would advance God's kingdom in the process! Keep God company; share in his work for his creation; do something every day to express his compassion. And just in case you say, 'I'm not in a position to do anything,' then remember that Trevor reported that one of the most inspiring people he has ever met, someone who has remained an inspiration to him for over 40 years, was an elderly woman confined to her bed in a psycho-geriatric hospital.

Then go back to the diary or chart and make a note of the circumstances of your action; what you did, how you felt, and how you think God would be thinking and feeling about your behaviour. If you mean to love yourself as you love your neighbour (to turn Leviticus 19.18 the other way round), then begin by loving your neighbour! Service of others brings its own rewards, and we begin to experience the abundant life God intends for us. Turning towards others can lead to our finding ourselves. It is the counter-intuitive nature of the gospel.

Evaluation

The point of experiments is not necessarily to prove something, but rather to tell us something. These experiments encourage us to test that the beliefs we hold about ourselves accord with the evidence we have about ourselves. We may start off thinking that our estimate of ourselves is absolutely true. However, in our evaluation of the experiments we will find that while bits of the evidence support our estimate, other elements question or contradict it. What this shows is that the belief that our beliefs should be held as absolute is disconfirmed. They are *not* absolutely true. Indeed, we human beings are never absolutely anything. Only God is absolute, and, thank God, God is absolute Love.

We therefore have a choice. If we prefer to think of ourselves as not much use and unattractive, we can; but this is not God's opinion of us, nor will the evidence wholly support it. Some of the time we may be a bit of a misery, but that is common to all of us. The evidence is that quite a few people think we are OK and so agree with God.

One final point

As we said in our opening chapter, some Christians are uncomfortable with all this attention on self. Is there not a danger that it can become a damaging preoccupation and encourage selfishness?

There are two responses to this. First, it depends on your motivation. If you think John was right when he spoke of Jesus wishing to give us abundant life, life at its fullest (John 10.10), and you think your life is not like that, with little of that abundance, then that seems to us to be a good enough reason to try the experiments we suggest.

Second, if you think you are not worth it, then by implication you are telling God that he got it wrong when he went to the effort of making you and loving you. Since God cannot be so mistaken, the misapprehension must be with you, and it is worth some effort to revise your thinking.

8

'It's all very well, but . . .'

Emotional inoculation

One of the reasons why life expectancy in affluent countries is higher than in the developing parts of the world is the wide spread use of inoculation – the health management practice employed when we know that children are going to be exposed to pathogens that lead to common childhood illnesses. By giving children an inoculation of small amounts of the pathogen doctors enable their immune systems to develop antibodies. When the exposure occurs, those antibodies do not necessarily stop the children getting the illness, but if they do fall ill, the symptoms will be much less harmful.

Now the previous chapters of this book have discussed changing our ways of thinking and behaving towards abundant living. Those of us who do so run the risk that at some time in the future an event or combination of events will occur that knocks us off balance, and we then slip back into our old habits. When this happens, it can for some be an enormous disappointment: 'I tried so hard. I thought I had beaten it, but here I am back, or even worse than I was before. I really should *not* love myself, it only leads to disappointment.'

So, in this final chapter let us think about a longer-term approach to coping, and let us first be realistic. The fact that we have acquired beneficial techniques of believing, behaving and thinking does not mean we are no longer susceptible to the negative events of life. They will continue to occur. But what has changed is that we have had an experience of things being different, and different because we have been active in making a difference. That experience of making a difference cannot be taken away from us, nor can the memory of it be obliterated. The evidence for our being back to where we were before is thus found wanting. At best it's inconclusive; in all probability it's simply untrue.

Yet while our negative belief about ourselves might have been undermined, we still remain vulnerable. What we need is an 'inoculation'.

This can come in two forms. The first involves taking a more pragmatic and objective look at our lives, thereby reducing the risk of surprise and unpreparedness. We need to give ourselves permission in advance to be sad if and when we suffer loss or unwanted change, or to be anxious and afraid when we are threatened.

We need to accept, also, that there will be occasions when coping will be more difficult simply because we are not equally competent at everything demanded of us. Some of us, when on a journey, seem to get lost quite easily, while others appear to be walking road maps. Some sing with effortless pitch and timing, even without much formal training, while others are, at best, confined to the joyful noise group. For some, managing their financial affairs appears to be as natural as breathing, for others it is a trauma that they avoid if they possibly can. For some, meeting new people is a joy that stimulates and enlivens them, while for others it is a chore.

The seasons and cycles of life provide another source of discomfort. We know of several gardeners who get feelings of depression between the end of September, when the nights get longer, and early February when the days lengthen and the soil begins to warm up. For others it is a cyclical routine at work that creates particularly stressful and unattractive tasks that have to be completed.

In the case of the inoculation of children against physical illness, parents need to accept the inevitable contact with the pathogen, and be prepared, with the doctor's help, to deal with it. Such acceptance is required of us in the case of our emotional inoculation.

In the 1990s a psychologist called Donald Meichenbaum developed an approach to psychological and emotional coping in which he emphasized the importance of how we have conversations with ourselves in our thinking. We have already spoken of these conversations in terms of 'self-speak'. We can reflect on the language we use and evaluate its truth (its evidence base) and its helpfulness. If we give ourselves a hard and abusive self-speak, loaded with guilt, blame, absolutes, imperatives, judgements, got tos and oughts, we are less likely to cope in a way that is helpful. Alternatively, if we develop in advance patterns or scripts of self-speak that are realistic and proportional, it becomes much easier to muster our resources to deal with bad things when they happen. We can reduce our anger, frustration or depression, and heighten our self-esteem. For Christians the knowledge of the love of God has a central role to play in this internal conversation, a love so passionate that it took him to Bethlehem and to Golgotha.

Creating a virtuous circle

Below are four examples of events that can have a negative influence on our well-being. Integral to each is the cycle of the Four Buttons, an idea introduced in Chapter 1 and referred to throughout this book. We would like you to try to see if you can identify, in each example, how the buttons can contribute to the creation of a vicious circle. Your task is then to experiment with means of changing, or working on one or more of the buttons, in order to create a *virtuous* circle.

1 Sometimes we have to behave in a way we don't like and that can seem out of character. Moments occur when we are different from our normal selves. It pays to think and be honest about what has changed in our lives. Even though we

think we are coping, such changes always have the potential to influence our response to events, particularly changes we might not welcome, such as doing exams, or searching for a job, facing excess pressures at work, or experiencing unemployment, unwanted retirement, not having enough to do. Wet weather might be keeping us off our beloved allotment or garden; engineering works might lead to the cancellation of our train, when we really do need to get to our destination by a certain time; a power cut might occur just as we are cooking for an important family get-together. These events will have an effect on all four buttons and the attendant feelings are normal and natural. The important task is to acknowledge the existence of the change and give ourselves permission to be different, even if only for a short while. Our initial responses may not be very desirable, but having them does not mean we are flawed; it simply shows us how normal we are.

2 Sometimes we experience significant biological events: we have a baby, or we catch flu, become immobilized, lose sensory information. And inevitably we get older, and many of us get old. Such events all have an effect on each of the four buttons, and feeling low or upset is often part of the process. We may need help if our responses cause particular difficulties, but their occurrence is part of life, not evidence of our being inadequate, let alone a sub-human being.

3 Most of us will experience loss or bereavement. When we mislay or lose a treasured possession that is enough to make us sad. If someone we love and have loved for many years dies, then we may experience the depths of bereavement with their attendant disorientation, disintegration and despair. There is a big black hole that feels like fear. This is normal for many animals; it is not restricted to human beings. It is well known that elephants grieve, but recent research has suggested that even geese may do so. For most of us it is a process, not a pathological condition. And love, understanding,

support and acceptance from those around us give us the means to live again without the person who was there before. C. S. Lewis' book *A Grief Observed* explores this concept of learning to live again and many people have found it very helpful. Yet grief can be so overwhelming, and for some it lasts so long, that we need here to spend a little time on it before we move on. And let's face it, the Church does not always help as much as it might.

A young woman – let us call her Dawn – died from cancer some years ago, when she was in her early twenties. She was a lovely, bubbly, very bright person, with a strong moral sense and a deep faith. She had to take a year out of university because of her illness, but with great courage she went back to finish her course, and remarkably gained a first-class degree. But she was not there at the graduation ceremony. She had died, and though her name was read out, her chair was empty. She and her equally lovely parents belonged to a small church community, and their building wasn't big enough for Dawn's funeral. They hired a large local hall, and it was packed with hundreds of mostly young people. There was a profound silence in the place, broken only by the small sound of tears. You could touch the grief. The service was far too long, taken by men in black suits, with no contribution from the family. One after another, these men, the elders of Dawn's church, paid tribute to her faith, and how it meant she was now in heaven with God, so all was well. We waited for the grief to be acknowledged, the brutal sense of loss; we waited for the word 'tragedy' to be said, because that is what her death felt like. We waited in vain. The service was a sham.

That is perhaps the worst example either of us has ex-perienced, yet it has become normal in recent decades in this country for a funeral service to be first and foremost a celebration of a person's life, perhaps exclusively so, with lots of alleluias in the hymns, and little space for the outpouring of grief. Those who take funerals are used to people *apologizing* afterwards for being upset! It is not their fault. It's the fault of our society, which finds grief difficult and turns it into an embarrassment. And it's the greater fault of the Church, which too often, to use the devastating words of Walter Brueggemann, 'goes on singing "happy songs" in the face of raw reality'.[17] Any faith that has the crucifixion of a good, very good, young man at its heart (to say the least of it) should be one that helps us all face reality, even when it is pitch black, not one that encourages us to deny it.

As we have already seen, the Bible does not deny it. Those dark prayers of lament, and often complaint, are everywhere in the Old Testament (which formed Jesus' Scriptures), while in Mark's and Matthew's Gospels, 'My God, my God, why have you forsaken me?' (a quotation of the beginning of Psalm 22) are the only words that the crucified Christ speaks from the cross. He hurls his pain, his bewilderment, his crushing loneliness into the dark, and then he dies. Only when reality is faced can resurrection happen. Of course, we have the love, understanding, support and acceptance of God always surrounding us, also. They are the stuff of the universe, its bright matter. Yet at times of great grief, as C. S. Lewis acknowledges so movingly in *A Grief Observed*, it sometimes seems we can't get through to God, that he is shutting us out, and it needs the persistent love of others to take us there and eventually show us the Truth again.

4 Most of us have known bereavement. Some of us have known worse. We have experienced trauma and/or abuse, and are living with its memory contaminating our lives. 'Why me?' we say. 'There must be something wrong with me for it to have happened to me.' Such thoughts are natural, because we hope to make sense of something that is incomprehensible. But although they may be natural and normal thoughts and questions, they are not helpful, because they cannot be answered. We cannot get inside the head of those who have

hurt us to understand their why. As frequently is the case with questions we cannot answer, we think that if only we try harder, and give the memories more attention, we will find the elusive solution. The consequence is, we dwell on what has happened to us and re-experience the attendant fear, disgust, pain, shame and guilt. Thus we feel helpless to change, or to make a difference, and we find ourselves condemned to relive what has been done to us for the rest of our lives. No wonder a common antecedent of depression is trauma and abuse. Not sin.

Yet some Christians will tell you that depression is a sin, or if they don't say that in so many words, they will make it plain enough that that is what they think. Millions of words have been written on the subject of depression, but as far as we are aware none of them speaks of people being *tempted* to be depressed. We can give ourselves permission to be depressed as a means of understanding why we have responded to events and circumstances in a particular way; but that empowers change. Depression can only be a sin if God commands us to be cheerful all the time. It might seem from some worship songs that he does, but their obligatory cheerfulness belongs to escapist religion, not to faith that is rooted in the realities of life (and death), and which is centred on the cross.

Having the blues . . . and a final word on the love of God

We have seen how what jazz calls 'the blues' is part of life. Sometimes it's a not very good day; at other times we are so low that it gets in the way of our living and interferes with our ability to love others. It can also be very distracting, but perversely paying it too much attention hinders rather than helps.

We have also seen that feeling low is often a normal response to events that happen. But these responses do not make us flawed or deeply faulted, and it is possible to experiment with ways that work for us and help us cope. Coping means we will feel better about ourselves and will be more effective in loving others.

'Love your neighbour as yourself,' says Leviticus. It is no accident that the writer puts love of self and love of neighbour together, nor that Jesus and Paul put such emphasis on these words. Jesus, according to Mark, Matthew and Luke, put those two loves beside another, the whole-hearted love of God. In doing so Jesus was following other Jewish teachers before him, who had already agreed that love of God, love of neighbour and love of self was what we might call a holy trinity of loves that went to the heart of the Jewish law and neatly expressed its purpose.

There is, however, another, much greater Love, the only love that fully deserves a capital letter, and that is the Love of God for us. On that all other loves depend. It is their starting point and their end. It calls all other loves into being, it is the air they breathe, and it is their destiny. All love begins with God bending over us, as he does in the Garden of Eden, to give us the kiss of life. And all love points towards the holy city, that new Jerusalem which comes 'down out of heaven from God, prepared as a bride adorned for her husband'. Notice the simile there, reflect on it for a moment, and then see how the writer of Revelation continues:

> See, the home of God is among mortals.
> He will dwell with them;
> they will be his peoples,
> and God himself will be with them;
> he will wipe every tear from their eyes.
> Death will be no more;
> mourning and crying and pain will be no more,
> for the first things have passed away.
>
> (Revelation 21.3–4)

After that, what is there to say?

Notes

1 Everett Fox, *The Five Books of Moses*, London: The Harvill Press, 1995, p. 603.
2 Fox, *Five Books of Moses*, p. 602.
3 Walter Brueggemann, *Praying the Psalms*, 2nd edition, Milton Keynes: Paternoster Press, 2007, p. 64.
4 Trevor Dennis, 'I do not need your grandeur', in *God in our Midst*, London: SPCK, 2012, p. 113.
5 Dennis, 'The child in the midst', in *God in our Midst*, p. 30.
6 From *Forms of Prayer for Jewish Worship*, Oxford: Oxford University Press, 1952, p. 8. Reproduced by kind permission of The Movement for Reform Judaism.
7 Trevor Dennis, *The Three Faces of Christ*, London: SPCK, 1999, pp. 86, 87–8.
8 The Anglican Church in Aotearoa, New Zealand and Polynesia, *A New Zealand Prayer Book – He Karakia Mihinare o Aotearoa*, London: Harper-Collins, 1997, p. 485.
9 From Holy Communion, Order One, Eucharistic Prayer A (and C). Extracts from *Common Worship: Services and Prayers for the Church of England* are copyright © The Archbishops' Council, 2000, and are reproduced by permission. <copyright@churchofengland.org>
10 From Hillsong, 'I could sing of your love forever'.
11 James L. Crenshaw, *Ecclesiastes: A Commentary*, London: SCM Press, 1988, pp. 57, 189. He discusses his translation on pp. 57–8.
12 Joel B. Green, *The Gospel of Luke*, Grand Rapids, MI: Eerdmans, 1997, p. 202.
13 From Dennis, *God in our Midst*, pp. 50–1; the quotation of Desmond Tutu is taken from his book, *No Future without Forgiveness*, London: Rider, 1999.
14 Josephus, *The Jewish War*, IV, ix, 1.
15 Megan McKenna, *Leave Her Alone*, New York: Orbis, 2000, p. 53.
16 Frances Taylor Gench, *Back to the Well*, Philadelphia, PA: Westminster John Knox Press, 2004, p. 96.
17 Walter Brueggemann, 'The Costly Loss of Lament', *JSOT* 36, 1986, p. 52.